Brothers and Sisters

Born to Bicker?

Pamela Shires Sneddon

Enslow Publishers, Inc.

40 Industrial Road · PO Box 38
Box 398 · Aldershot
Berkeley Heights, NJ 07922 · Hants GU12 6BP
USA · UK

http://www.enslow.com

Dedicated to my daughter Stephanie Sneddon, for reading every page I wrote— and making many helpful suggestions!

Copyright © 1996 by Pamela Shires Sneddon

Library of Congress Cataloging-in-Publication Data

Sneddon, Pamela Shires.
    Brothers and sisters: born to bicker / Pamela Shires Sneddon
        p. cm. — (Teen Issues)
    Includes bibliographical references and index.
    Summary: Explores various aspects of sibling relationships, including how rivalry, birth order, and growing up affect how siblings interact with each other.
    ISBN 0-89490-914-2
    1. Brothers and sisters—Juvenile literatures. 2. Sibling rivalry—Juvenile literature. [1. Brothers and sisters. 2. Sibling rivalry.] I. Title. II. Series.
    BF723.S43S64   1997
    306.875—dc20   96-32677
                                                                    CIP
                                                                    AC

Printed in the United States of America

10 9 8 7 6 5 4 3

Cover Illustration: Pamela Shires Sneddon

This is a superb book for all members of the family—especially teens who want to make some sense out of their relationships with brothers and sisters. Packed with up-to-date information that will surprise and enlighten, *Brothers and Sisters: Born to Bicker?* is appealing reading and is filled with useful suggestions for understanding and improving these important family connections.

—Stephen P. Herman, M.D.
Associate Clinical Professor of Psychiatry
Yale University Child Study Center

Contents

Author's Note

All of the incidents and quotations in this book are from real life. Many of the quotes are from students at Santa Barbara High School who both spoke with me and filled out a questionnaire. (To protect their privacy, the names of these students have been changed in many cases.) I also talked to specialists in the field who kindly shared their insights as well as some of their research results with me. Several of the examples used are from the siblings I grew up with—my sister and brothers—and the ones I see interact every day—my children.

1

Brothers and Sisters—
Relationships for Life

□ Laetitia leaned forward, her face tightening with anger. "My sister took my skirt and didn't even ask, then when she brought it back, she left it crumpled on the floor. She knows I hate that!"

□ "My little brother is totally spoiled," volunteered Tracy. "He gets to do whatever he wants."

□ José said, "My older brother told me he'd rather give money to a dog than to me."

□ "Every time a guy likes me, my sister tries to take him away. She can't even let me have a boyfriend." Sarah's eyes showed the hurt even as she tried to laugh.

These teens are caught in the cross fire of a common battleground: sibling rivalry and conflict. Almost everyone has a sibling, a brother or sister, but most of us just live through the day-to-day ups and downs of the relationship without understanding its effects. As one sixteen-year-old said about his sister: "I grew up with her and that's about it."

In the past, even those who study family relationships did not pay much attention to the interaction between brothers and sisters. Only in recent years have experts realized that the sibling relationship has much to do with how we feel about ourselves, as well as how we relate to others throughout our lives.

Is Sibling Rivalry a Fact of Life?

Does there have to be sibling rivalry? Can sisters be friends even though they're different? Will a little brother always be a pest? Insights from experts and teenagers themselves show that sibling rivalry is only one part of the sibling experience, that differences are to be expected, and that the relationship changes over time. Even little brothers grow up!

While there are siblings who seem to mirror the *Brady Bunch*, and some who are more like the *Addams Family*, most brother and sister relationships have elements of both. Dr. Gene Brody of the University of Georgia says, "A typical sibling relationship is a mix: lots of positivity, lots of negativity, and lots of emotionality. What undergirds it is a caring for the brother or sister."[1]

LaToya, sixteen and the youngest of five, agrees. "My family is kind of like the Cosbys on TV. We get in fights, then we get along. It's a challenge, but I love them all."

Even in a healthy family, however, this love might not be obvious. A family counselor commented, "If you asked a teen if she still loved the sister who borrowed her jeans and put a hole in them, it would be 'I hate her!' There is a lot of love, but it's way down there. It's not at all conscious a lot of the time."[2]

Jimmy, fifteen, now jokes about this memory, but it wasn't funny when it happened: "I remember I used to fall off my bike—my brothers were teaching me to ride—and they'd *laugh* at me and I'd be crying."

However hurtful it is to have older brothers laughing at your failures or a sister using your closet like her own or even trying to move in on your boyfriend, there are many good things about having a sibling. Twin brothers Albert and Allen Hughes, who released their first feature film, *Menace II Society*, when they were twenty-one, rely on each other's strengths. "The best thing about my brother," said Albert in a 1993 magazine interview, "is that he's there for me."[3]

Experts find many benefits in having brothers and sisters: One calls the sibling relationship an "apprenticeship for life." Another sees it as a preparation for marriage. Still another says it is "a bridge to peer relationships." Dr. Paul Meisel says that kids with brothers or sisters "have a huge leg up on social relationships over only children."[4]

Most teens would agree. Out of ninety-five high-school students questioned, eighty-seven had positive things to say about having siblings.[5]

"My sister is probably the only person who knows almost everything about me," says Emily, eighteen.

Cheering for the Home Team

Siblings can also serve as cheerleaders for each other, as this true story illustrates:

Luke, eleven, was taking part in his school track meet. His mother wasn't feeling well so his older brother Mike, seventeen, took their six-year-old brother, Tony, and went to pick Luke up. The two brothers got to the school in time to see Luke run in his last race.

Their mother was in the kitchen when all three brothers returned and burst into the house, Mike and Tony talking at the same time in their excitement, Luke grinning from ear to ear.

"Oh, Mom! You should have seen it," said Mike. "Luke was awesome! Here, let me show you." Mike grabbed the salt and pepper shakers and crashed them down on the table. "Okay, they start out—there're about fifteen of them and Luke is back there"—Mike put the salt shaker in the back to indicate Luke's position—"they're running, they're running, and Luke is still back there and here are the guys in front." Mike waved the pepper shaker in his left hand to show the front-runners. "Now, here comes Luke." He moved the salt shaker forward. "He's pulling up, he's pulling up, and at the last second, he moves ahead!" He made the salt shaker victoriously pass the pepper shaker.

The brothers jubilantly gave each other high fives, while Luke, smiling self-consciously, shook his head. He didn't say anything, but his eyes were shining: clearly this was a moment he'd always remember. Only later did their mother find out that Luke had come in fourth. For Luke, thanks to his brothers, it was as big a victory as if he'd won first place.

"The best thing about having a sibling is having a friend to go home to," adds Joe, fifteen.

Others appreciated having someone to confide in. Caroline, fifteen, says, "If you have a brother or sister, you have someone whom you can trust to talk with and share things."

Susan, fifteen, finds that siblings give a fresh perspective on life: "Having two brothers has helped me to see how different people react to different things."

Michael, fourteen, depends on his siblings for support: "They're fun to have when you're either lonely or very sad, and they do help you a lot when you're in trouble."

The Benefits of Siblings

Studies have shown that having a brother or sister in the same school as you can be a big help, especially during the adjustment period. Vanessa, fourteen, likes it that her sister helps her with schoolwork, while Sean, fourteen, says that from his brother, he learns things and knows the hip styles.

Older brothers and sisters are powerful role models. A 1991 study suggested that an admired and stable older brother can have a protective influence against drug use in a more risk-prone younger brother.[6] One teen commented, "If it weren't for my brothers, I would probably be in a gang."

Siblings often support each other when their parents are in conflict or fail to provide a nurturing environment. Tawni and Phil provide an extreme example of what this can mean. Tawni had run away at fourteen from an abusive, alcoholic mother. She was able to finish high school at the age of fifteen and found help to attend the University of California at Santa Barbara, where she graduated at age nineteen. One year earlier, when she was eighteen, preparing for her senior year of college, she took in her younger brother, Phil, who had fled home just as she had four years earlier. Tawni was carrying a full load of classes and working part-time. "It was scary," she said. "But I wanted to help him excel. People did that for me. I wanted to do the same for my brother." In 1995, Phil graduated from high school with good grades and a place in a state college for the fall.[7]

While Tawni and Phil's story might be unusual, experts agree that the sibling relationship is not to be taken for granted. "It is going to be the one that you take throughout your life, and it's going to last longer than all your others, including your spousal relationship. So it's something to nurture," says Dr. Brody.[8] A family counselor puts it this way: "Sometimes you think you will never like your brother or sister, but there is no one else who will share the same memory bank. A sibling can be a resource for life."[9]

How can you put this resource to work for you—and for your sibling? First, it helps to understand what goes into forging the sibling bond as well as what splits it apart. In the next chapters of this book, you will be able to look at some of the things that affect how you feel about your sibling or siblings. Perhaps, as you look at these factors and read about the experiences of others, you will be encouraged to consider ways to help improve your own sibling relationship so that you and your brother or sister can be there for each other in the years ahead.

Test Your S.I.Q.*

(Sibling Intelligence Quotient)

1. **A sibling is:**
   a. a small piece of chicken.
   b. a part of a sentence.
   c. a brother or sister.

2. **Your sister and you might be described as having a roller-coaster relationship—sometimes you're best friends and sometimes you can't stand her. This means you:**
   a. have a terrible sister.
   b. are a terrible person.
   c. have a normal sibling relationship.

3. **One of the benefits of having a brother or sister is:**
   a. having someone to beat up on.
   b. getting to blame things on him or her.
   c. learning to get along with another person.

4. **You go to your little brother's game and tell him what a great job he did, even though his team loses. You:**
   a. are overdoing the flattery.
   b. should have told him what he did wrong.
   c. gave him a great gift no one else can give—your approval.

5. **You are mad at your sister for borrowing your jeans without asking. You:**
   a. will always hate her.
   b. shouldn't get mad.
   c. still can love her even if you are angry.

Answers on Page 110

2

Setting the Stage for Sibling Rivalry

People living in the same environment can expect to have some conflict. Different temperaments, different expectations of each other—often just wanting the same object—can cause strife. For siblings there is another issue: rivalry. This can mean rivalry for their parents' attention and love or rivalry for status in the outside world.

As the following comments of Betty and Penny illustrate, there are problems that occur when siblings are fairly close in age, like Penny and her sister Mary, and problems that arise when there is a large age gap, as in the case of Betty and her little sister. While Betty's mother, like most parents, would like to think that being sisters should keep them from fighting, it is unrealistic to expect things to always go smoothly in families.

My little sister? She's six. I swear, she's, like, mean. We just don't like each other at all. There's no way. My mom doesn't understand that. My little sister will walk by me and I'll just look at her and she'll hit me. My mom's all: "You guys are sisters, you shouldn't be fighting." I'm all: "She started it!" And they always blame it on me!

—Betty, fourteen

I get mad when my twelve-year-old sister Mary wants to get the same outfit I'm buying. Like, I'll tell her off and take the clothes from her and throw them on the ground and say, "You're not getting these clothes because I'm getting them instead!"

—Penny, sixteen

However, there are families in which rivalry and conflict are minimal. Courtney, fifteen, talks about the relationship she has with her three sisters—ages thirty-two, thirty, and seventeen—as being very, very close. She says, "My oldest sister is like a second mom to me, and the next one down always makes me laugh. My seventeen-year-old sister is my best friend."

In other families, there is a high level of anger and bitterness. Esther, eighteen, comments, "I can't ever remember a good time with my brother."

What Causes Conflicts?

Sibling rivalry especially stands out in families in which there is not a lot of parental affirmation and love. Dr. Dean Given, family counselor, has compared this situation to a person dealing with a bank account. He says, "If there isn't much money in your account, you watch it with a lot more attention than when it's full. If there's plenty of money, you can let a few statements go, but if it's real close and tight, then you have to watch it carefully. So if it's real close and tight with Mom and she notices your brother's paper as being good, then you [feel jealous] and rivalry clearly exists."[1]

Areas of conflict and rivalry change with age. Young children compete for Mom and Dad's attention and love: "Look at me, Mom!" or "I want to sit on your lap, too!" a six-year-old might cry. When that six-year-old enters his teenage years, Mom and Dad's approval is still important, but now he measures himself against others, including his sibling, in the areas of athletic ability, grades, appearance, and social success.

Henry, sixteen, finds it frustrating that his parents seem to value his younger brother's artistic talents more than they do Henry's musical ability. Penny's

To understand the causes of sibling rivalry and conflict, it will help to look at several influential factors that provide the backdrop for sibling rivalry. These include:

- ❏ birth order
- ❏ gender
- ❏ age spacing
- ❏ sibling access
- ❏ family roles
- ❏ ethnic, cultural, religious, and economic effects
- ❏ genetic and environmental influences

angry feelings against Mary, who wants to get the same outfit, stem from wanting to be unique but also might reflect competition with her sister in appearance.

Birth Order. There are three basic positions for children in a family: oldest, middle, and youngest. These positions in the family are what is meant by birth order. There are variations since, for example, being the youngest of two is different than being the youngest of four or more, and a middle child of three has a different position than a middle child where there are six children in the family. The effect of birth order has received much attention in recent years, with studies indicating that children in each position tend to share certain characteristics. Oldest children are often perfectionistic, reliable, serious, critical, and well organized. They tend to buy into the family values and to be more parental. They are the ones who have to break the ice for younger siblings. Middle children have a little more trouble finding their place, but they often have lots of friends and do well in life because they are born negotiators. Youngest children tend to experience their parents as more relaxed, but they often feel they are not taken seriously. They might be manipulative, but they are outgoing and can become the clowns of the family.[2]

Like most generalizations, this theory does not fit every family, and it is only one of many factors to be considered. However, comments from several teenagers show that birth order does affect how individuals see themselves. David, fifteen and an oldest child, calls himself "the serious one who always takes charge." Amber, fourteen and also the oldest, feels responsible for the effect her actions have on the rest of the family: "I try to be a good role model for my little brother," she says.

Luis, fifteen, is in the middle and sees himself as "the funny person and the crazy one" of the family. Another middle child, Terry, fourteen, feels that she is the one who gets in trouble the most.

As the youngest in her family, De'Ardra, fourteen, says she is "the only one who can get away with things; the baby."

Gender. Another factor affecting sibling relationships is gender—whether one is male or female. For example, one study has shown that female siblings tend to be better than male siblings in teaching a simple task to younger brothers and sisters. Males find teaching younger, unrelated children easier than working with their own brothers and sisters.[3] Another study found that school-age sisters play together more than brothers do.[4] Rivalry is usually less intense between different-sex siblings and most intense in two-child families of boys.[5]

The way in which parents treat each sibling can be affected by gender. If Dad is not at ease with girls and has daughters or Mom did not grow up with brothers and has sons, Dad can find himself more comfortable relating to his son and Mom to her daughter.[6] A 1976 study of mother-child interaction found that mothers tend to help younger children more when the oldest sibling is a male.[7]

Gender also affects birth order characteristics. For example, if the first child is a boy and the second a girl, each would share characteristics of a first-born because each would be the oldest of their sex. If the first child is a boy, the next a girl, and the next also a girl, then the middle child has undergone a dramatic role change in the family. She is no longer the only girl and she is no longer the youngest.

Age Spacing. Age spacing—how many years separate siblings—is important to their later relationship. If they are less than two years apart, siblings have no remembrance of being an only child. Although siblings two years or less apart can be playmates for each other, there is often greater quarreling and antagonism. There are also problems when the younger brother or sister has a greater ability in one area than the older sibling.

An example of this is the situation that existed with Marie and Ellen. Marie was a year and a half older than her sister Ellen. When she was six, Marie received a new bicycle. Even with her parents' help, it was several weeks before she finally learned to ride. That same day, as Marie laid the bike down, her little sister Ellen picked it up, hopped on, and rode off—her first time on the bike. Even in her thirties, Marie remembered how her little sister's superior physical ability made her feel.

Sam's brother Mac is two years younger than Sam, but now Mac is only an inch shorter and twenty pounds heavier than fifteen-year-old Sam. As Sam says, "the competition is getting greater than it was before."

Another difficulty can arise with closely spaced siblings when the older sibling begins to get more privileges. Jenny, eleven, and Nancy, twelve, are two sisters who were very close until this year. Now Jenny resents the fact that Nancy is allowed to do more.[8] Scott, fifteen, says: "I get to do a lot more than my brother, who is two years younger. My parents say to

Playing a Part

When a hundred high-school students were asked to describe their roles in the family, most of them quickly saw themselves in relation to their brothers and sisters:

☐ *My sister is the level-headed one who is always organized. I'm spontaneous and energetic.*

—Will, fourteen

☐ *I'm the bad girl, my sister is the good girl.*

—Lorena, fourteen

☐ *I am the she-looks-just-like-her-older-sister and the why-can't-you-get-good-grades-like-her one. The in-between smart and can't be stupid. The hypochondriac. The stubborn one. The one who always goes through phases.*

—Barbara, fourteen

☐ *My role is to set the example for my brother and sister. I need to get good grades in school and can't do anything wrong.*

—Blanca, fifteen

☐ *As my family says, I'm the trouble-maker.*

—Sonia, fourteen

☐ *The twenty-one-year-old is serious, but teddy-bear-like, comforting. The eighteen-year-old is the "problem child," does what he wants. I'm the neutral one—the* Star Trek *freak.*

—Kellie, fifteen

☐ *I'm smart, she's smarter. I'm funny, she tries to be funny.*

—Brian, fifteen

☐ *My oldest brother is the one who comes up with get-rich-quick schemes, and my second oldest brother is the rebel who has tattoos and rides Harleys. I don't really know who I am.*

—Emily, fourteen

Thad, 'He's older than you,' and he gets frustrated because I'm not that much older."

With more than a two-year age gap between brothers and sisters, there is less competition with the older brother or sister; in fact, often the older one becomes almost like another parent. Terry, fourteen, and the middle of eight children, says she just likes spending time with her two little sisters (three-year-old twins) and her little brother (age ten). For some, however, as is shown in the relationship between Betty and her little sister (see p. 15), younger siblings just bug!

What underlies much of the irritation with the bugging is that young children are very intrusive into older children's lives. They get into things and they take up space and they are not held accountable because they are too little. Meanwhile, the older child is held accountable for those very situations.[9] As Betty said in frustration, "And they always blame it on me!"

Sibling Access. The term *sibling access* means the number of common life events siblings encounter together. Psychologists Dr. Stephen Bank and Dr. Michael Kahn found that similarity in age and sex promotes access, and differences in age and sex diminish it. They say: "Siblings who are high in access have often attended the same schools, played with the same friends, dated in the same crowd, been given a common bedroom (even the same bed), worn each other's clothes, and so on."[10]

Siblings who spend a great deal of time together when they are young children have more of an impact on each other's personalities than children who do not spend time together in the early years. The earlier access begins, and the more prolonged it is, the more intense will be the relationship when the siblings face stresses in later life.[11]

Family Roles. The roles in a family are the parts each family member plays as he or she interacts with other family members. When one member of the family steps out of his or her role, it really affects the whole family. Of course, no one sits down when they decide to have children and says, "Now, we'll have three kids. Nell will be the quiet one who takes responsibility well, Fred will be the social one who gets along with everyone, and Linda will be the one who's always in trouble." Roles evolve over time and are affected by all the other background factors as well as personality and temperament.

Ethnic, Cultural, Religious, and Economic Effects. We do not live as isolated family units, but as part of an ethnic, cultural, religious, and economic network. These elements directly and indirectly affect our sibling relationships. In some cultures or religions, education might be stressed for boys and not for girls,[12] boys might be allowed more independence than girls, or one member of the family might be chosen to receive more of the family resources in order to succeed as the family representative.[13]

Economic factors can be interrelated with a family's cultural or ethnic background. Sharing housing with extended family could be culturally accepted or encouraged, or it might be from financial necessity alone. Both Lola and Barbara, teenagers from different families, share bedrooms with their aunts. This is a financial necessity, but it is also common in their culture, where family ties are very important. For Lola, it has been a positive experience; for Barbara, although she loves her aunt, it has been difficult.

José

American-born children of immigrant parents have additional adjustments, as this example shows:

José is the youngest in his family and the only child of seven siblings to be born in America. Initially exposed only to the ways of his family's culture, José felt secure and happy until he turned six and entered school. There he suffered an unfortunate cultural impact that confused and disturbed him.

"The first thing I learned when I started school," says José, "was that I was Mexican. Up until that time, I was never aware of this—that I was 'different' from those around me." As he became more at home in the American culture, he felt a separation from his parents as well as from his siblings, who were more comfortable with the ways of their country of origin.

"As I started to assimilate into American society, I began to experience embarrassment for my culture," explains José. "I tried to distance myself from the 'old' Mexican ways of my family. As I began to feel ashamed of my family, they began to feel ashamed of me, their 'American' child."

Later, José came to appreciate his heritage and the struggles his parents and his older siblings had made to adjust to a new country. Through his studies, he saw that many of the adjustments his family had faced were shared by immigrants from other countries in past years.[14]

Speaking about the effects of crowded living conditions on the sibling relationship, one expert sees a closeness of bonding within the family for better or for worse: it is just taken for granted that this is the way people are in families. He says, "Kids feeling that bond, well, there's a closeness that I think is very precious."[15]

On the other hand, when people live in crowded conditions, the level of conflict tends to go up. As teen counselor Stan Speck put it, "When there aren't a lot of rooms available and everybody's kind of smooshed together, there aren't a lot of boundaries. It's not to say people can't live that way and have healthy lives, it's just that there are more opportunities in some respects for boundaries to be crossed."[16]

One of the most critical impacts of today's economic situation has been the steady increase of both parents working. One counselor comments: "The impact is that with both parents working, there is little energy or time when they are home to give to kids. They take shortcuts to end conflict without resolving it."[17]

Genetic and Environmental Influences. Genetic influences are what a person inherits from his or her parents: brown eyes, curly hair, long or short legs, as well as how an individual is wired inside. Dr. Given says, "Some people are up and responsive, and their nervous system is such that they're going to be firing in a different way than someone who just floats through life without anything being a big challenge."[18]

Except in the case of identical twins, each of us has a different genetic makeup from everyone else. Dr. Shirley McGuire of the University of California at San Diego notes, "In general, siblings are not that much alike. If you think it's odd that you're different from your sibling, it's not. It's usually the norm."[19]

When people talk about environment, they are referring to our surroundings—physical and emotional. Physically, siblings might share the same parents, home, number of books on the shelf, and neighborhood, but each sibling looks at that environment in a different way.[20] And, depending on the age spacing, for many siblings the physical environment is not the same: parents are older, perhaps the financial situation is different. At a family gathering, the adult Hudson siblings were having a friendly argument. Anne and Jane were remembering their mother making breakfast for them before they left for school. Their brothers, Mike and Dave, argued that their father always made breakfast and especially remembered his corn pancakes. They were both right. When Anne and Jane were small, their mother did not work outside the home. After Michael and Dave were born, however, things changed. The family had moved to a large house in the country and their mother had returned to teaching. During this period, their father made breakfast so that their mother could get ready for work. For Dave and Michael, the family environment was different than it had been for the older sisters, including memories of family breakfasts.

Getting Closer

Explore Your Family Relationships

1. Make a chart of your family. List the name of each sibling, their place in the birth order, their gender, the age gap between the next older sibling and the next younger sibling, and their role in the family. Example:

Name	Birth Order	Gender	Age gap with older	Age gap with younger	Family Role
Anne	oldest	female	0 yrs	5 yrs	serious one
Jane	middle	female	5 yrs	1 yr	helpful
Mike	youngest	male	1 yr	0 yrs	funny

2. Make an environmental checklist. Give each of your siblings a piece of paper. Ask each one to list five things that stand out about your home. Then compare to see how you each see your environment in a different way. Example:

Anne   lots of rooms
dishes in sink

Jane   piano in living room
bush with yellow flowers outside front door

Mike   kids' trikes in driveway
next-door neighbor's Porsche

3

The Childhood Foundation

A couple, both psychologists, were expecting their second child. They had researched studies that showed the importance of age spacing on the sibling relationship and the fact that competition is greater when children are two years or less apart. They had also read that siblings too far apart in age miss out on shared experiences that would have made them closer. As a result, the new baby was arriving on schedule three years after the first. The parents had done all the things as suggested by studies showing that the more preparation an older child has for a new sister or brother, the smoother the adjustment is and the less sense of loss the older child experiences. "Yes," they told their three-year-old daughter, "there's a baby growing in Mommy's tummy," and "We love you and we'll love the new baby." They did everything they could think of to make it an easy transition: "Mommy was away and now Mommy's come home," they said after the birth of the new baby. They put the baby in the crib, picked up the three-year-old, and carried her over to see her new brother. She took one look into the crib and said, "Hate baby." As Dr. Given says, "This clearly shows sibling rivalry is no fantasy. The sense of loss experienced by the appearance of a new brother or sister on the scene is very real."[1]

"When you have a second child," adds Dr. Meisel, "there's a question to be dealt with, although it's probably not expressed, and that is: 'Why did you need another one—wasn't I enough?' The answer is, of course, 'No, you were not enough, I did need another one.'"[2]

Future Benefits of Current Conflict

However, there are benefits in childhood sibling rivalry and conflict. One expert says that by recognizing rivalry as neither bad nor good but just "is," parents have an opportunity to teach their children about living with other people in a benign setting, their home, before they have to learn it in the outside world where people might not be so supportive.[3]

"Having siblings has helped me at work," says Emily. "I know how to deal with people when they're annoying from dealing with my brothers."

"Just so," says Dr. Shirley McGuire. "In a work situation, you are with people you didn't pick, people who aren't necessarily friends, but you have to get along."[4]

Children learn how to negotiate and work out

differences. They learn to share resources, whether of things or their parents' attention. Children learn they are important, but not the only important one. They have to deal with concepts of fairness, with the bugging of younger siblings, or the resentment felt when older siblings get something that they don't. Children experience the use and abuse of power.[5] Conflict with brothers and sisters can teach which ways of expressing frustration work and which don't. Siblings learn how to deal with differences or resolve them and how to express anger and resolve it. The sibling relationship also gives the potential for loyalty in spite of conflict; the loyalty that says, "I can't stand my brother, but don't you pick on him!"[6]

If sibling rivalry and conflict are such good things, then why is there so much effort to combat them—besides the fact that it drives parents crazy? Just as the seeds for later good relationships are sown in childhood sibling interaction, those that will develop into harmful and negative relationships are also planted. For example, there seems to be a strong link between hostile sibling contact and later poor marital relationships.[7] Most experts agree that it is not the conflict itself that is the culprit. Problems arise when there are only fights and no warmth in the relationship.

Furthermore, many things children learn from sibling conflict are not always skills that are desirable.[8] Children are often poor problem solvers,[9] and the strategies they use to solve the conflict may be the same ones that got them into opposition in the first place. What children need are adults to explain to them what strategy worked in a situation or why it did not and to provide some of the explanation that goes along with the strategies they are using.[10]

How Parents Affect Sibling Relationships

What all experts agree on is the importance of parents in the sibling relationship—more important than all of the background factors that were discussed in the previous chapter. Parents have the most impact on how their children relate to one another in two ways. First in importance to the sibling bond is the quality of each parent's relationship with the other. Second, parents influence sibling interaction by the way each parent relates with each child in the family.

The place to begin is with the parents' own relationship. A warm, loving, and mutually supportive mother and father provide the best foundation for a place in which each sibling feels secure and loved. On the other hand, when parents are constantly fighting, children's emotional security is undermined, hurting their ability to function socially and to control their behavior with siblings.[11]

Resolution Is Key

Except for abusive physical or verbal behavior, conflict between parents is not in itself destructive. Resolution is the key to both modeling behavior for children and reinforcing their security so that they will be able to develop healthy interaction with their siblings, as well as future relationships.

Several studies have shown that children's responses to fights that were resolved were very different from their reactions to unresolved conflict.[12] Children benefit the most if adults show that compromise, apology, and getting back together after an argument are the way to handle disagreements. However, even if adults make up in private, children tend to feel that the general atmosphere in the family is good.[13]

Unexpressed conflict that is under the surface, as in families where "we never argue" is the rule, can have damaging results. Children learn that emotions are not to be expressed, and they do not have models for how to deal with the anger they might feel for a sibling. They may not learn that you can love a person and still argue. Or, as in the following family, the siblings may fight as fill-ins for the parents. A family with four daughters came for counseling. One of the family rules was no fighting, for which the parents set the example. In spite of this rule, the two youngest daughters, ten and twelve, quarreled all the time. Although all the family members had another reason for why this went on, it was obvious that one girl was on her father's side and the other identified with her mother. Whenever it seemed that the parents might disagree, the two girls started fighting. It turned out, in fact, that the parents had serious issues that were upsetting to them, but they had not directly confronted each other because they were afraid of the results. When they were able to talk openly to each other and found that they could survive a quarrel, the atmosphere in the family cleared and the younger sisters stopped their incessant fighting.[14]

If parents have ongoing fights and arguments that are not resolved, then the feelings of anger and resentment can spill over into each parent's relationship with each child and make that relationship more negative. This in turn spills over into the sibling relationship. When there is this chronic conflict, parents are also more likely to treat their children differently, which, as will be shown later, is an underlying cause of sibling rivalry.[15]

In addition to the parent-parent relationship, how each parent treats each child is of foremost importance to the sibling relationship. A psychologist says that when people come to him because their children are not getting along, he finds it much more helpful to have parents start looking at their relationship with each child rather than focusing only on what is going on between the kids.[16] One study found that families in which the mothers enjoyed their maternal role and encouraged openness and curiosity in their children, without resorting to threats or harsh physical control, had less conflict between siblings. The children also got along better with others outside the family.[17]

The importance of the mother-child relationship has long been known. What was a surprise to Dr. Brody was the importance of the father's role in sibling interaction. This expert felt that since fathers in our society are generally scarcer resources than mothers, perhaps the things that happen with fathers are psychologically more impressive for kids. "The message this sends to me," he says, "is that fathers had better be there for their children. Not only will this affect their own individual development, but the role a father has with each child will play a prominent part in the kind of relationship children build with each other."[18]

There is no one way to raise healthy, loving children. The quality of the emotional relationships between the parents and between the parent and child are more important than strategies and techniques.[19] However, the way parents deal with the issues of fairness, comparisons, and disputes between siblings are major factors in defusing or escalating sibling rivalry and conflict.

A Question of Fairness

"It's not fair! It's not fair! Mark got a pizza and I didn't!"

Trying to be fair—doing exactly the same thing for each child in a family—is almost impossible. Family counselor Hanne Sonquist suggests it is better to try to be sensitive to individual needs. "For example," she says, "buying a new shirt for each of two kids, even though one of the kids doesn't care at all about it and the other one has really wanted a new shirt, might be fair but does not meet each child's needs." Parents may have more finances available at certain times and not at others. If a child feels unfairly treated, a parent can ask, "How would you see it as fair? What could we do to make it better?"[20]

One expert said, "What we typically find is that parents don't treat the children the same. They love them equally, but they will tell you honestly that they might have to discipline one more, they might have to hug another one more, another one needs a little more support. In a healthy family, the kids don't notice any really big difference or feel unloved."[21]

In the Benson family there is a wide age space. The older children, including Mark, get more fringe benefits. The younger ones know they had better not touch the pizzas in the freezer or their older brother will come down hard on them. They might complain about it and say that it is unfair, but they really don't make a big fuss because they know that when they get to be teenagers,

The Effect of Comparisons

☐ "My parents are always comparing us: 'Marie always got straight A's, why can't you?'" says Nate, fifteen.

☐ "Comparison: it gets you to rebel," adds Sean, fifteen.

☐ "You could call making comparisons a formula for sibling conflict," agrees Hanne Sonquist.[22]

Although a natural tendency in most families is to compare one sibling's accomplishments to another's, this has a negative effect on both the disparaged child's self-esteem and the sibling relationship itself. Each child in a family should be recognized individually.[23]

A more subtle form of comparison occurs when a parent compliments an achievement or attribute of one sibling while speaking to another. An example of this would be a mother who might say to Nancy, who knows how important musical ability is to her mother: "Doesn't your sister Mary have a great voice? I just love to hear her sing!" What Nancy, who lacks this ability, hears is: "Your voice doesn't quite measure up," or "I value Mary's ability more than yours."

they will get more things, including pizzas. Of course, this would not work well in a family with children close in age. In that case, some other method, such as taking turns for special treats, would need to be used.

When there is extreme differential treatment and the kids know it, then there are problems. When one parent clearly prefers one child over another in the family, the one who is favored feels better about herself or himself, while the less favored one feels worse and has more behavior problems. For both children, however, the sibling relationship is terrible.[24]

The Handling of Disputes

Clearly, as much as parents would like it to be otherwise, brothers and sisters experience disputes early on. The way in which parents deal with these disputes in childhood makes a big difference in how brothers and sisters feel about each other in later life. The ideal atmosphere, according to experts is one in which parents will monitor squabbles, are emotionally accessible, can serve as a court of last resort, and model adequate conflict resolution.[25] Dr. John Platt, author and family counselor, feels that while this is the ideal atmosphere, the reality is that kids still do a lot of fighting, particularly if they are close in age. And, he says, it is often the older one who is punished, although both kids were equally involved. He advises staying out of the fights as much as possible, while making it clear that fighting is not a good solution or one of which the parents approve.[26] Parents can also try to minimize situations that tend to cause conflict and to create an environment that is not going to encourage it.[27]

One psychologist calls sibling disputes "opportunities for learning."[28] Young children, who pretty much learn by doing, can establish their own frame of reference for handling later problems by how they resolved their sibling battles as they were growing up. As an example of what this can mean, the following offers a look at a real-life situation.

Ten-year-old twins Andrew and Russell were getting their own breakfasts while their mother showered. Holding a bowl of Cheerios and milk, Russell was standing in front of the pantry reading the cereal box. Andrew bumped him as he went past, sending wet Cheerios and milk flying onto the pantry shelves and dripping down to the floor. Russell turned around and threw what was left of the cereal at his brother, splattering Andrew, the cupboards, and the floor on the other side of the kitchen with the soggy mess.

"I'm telling!" Andrew yelled and ran down the hallway to stand outside the bathroom door. Russell joined him, and both brothers shouted over the shower's noise at their mother. She emerged from the bathroom in her robe and stalked out to the kitchen, where she stood looking at the scene silently. Each brother told his version of the incident while blaming the other one at the top of his voice: "Andrew pushed me!" "Russ threw the cereal at me!" Their mother waited until they stopped, then said, "This is a mess. I am not very happy about it. We are leaving for school in fifteen minutes and it had better be cleaned up before we go. I'm going to get dressed."

When she came back out to the kitchen, the boys

were talking together amicably as they got their backpacks ready. The cereal and milk were cleaned up, even though the floor was still a little sticky. Their mother told them that she appreciated how well they had worked together to solve the problem.

What did Andrew and Russell learn from this "opportunity"? First, they had to work together to come up with a solution to a dispute, regardless of who felt who had started it. They had to mop up each area, and during the process they were able to get rid of their anger with each other and move on. Their mother helped them by allowing them to express their feelings without her comment and without involving her as judge. Her confidence in their ability to solve the problem showed that she valued them as individuals.

A Matter of Temperament

While background factors help explain some aspects of the sibling relationship and parents have the primary role in guiding them, there are other factors to be considered, the most important of which is temperament. Temperament is the typical way an individual emotionally responds to a situation. The dominant quality of each person's temperament is one of the things that makes one person different from another.

"Temperament," says Dr. Meisel, "is one of the few factors that tends to be reliably seen as inherited, but not inherited like eye color because it is malleable. That is, if you take a child with a placid and easygoing temperament and put him in a very hyperactive kind of family, the child changes more toward acting like the rest of the family. But very early, before birth order could have any effect, you see the differences in temperament in kids."[29]

These differences can affect the way siblings react with each other. For example, children with highly active and emotionally intense temperaments, who are often thought of as "difficult," tend to experience conflict in their relationships both inside and outside the family.[30]

Siblings have a powerful impact on the temperament of their brothers and sisters. In fact, the child psychiatrist Dr. Rudolph Dreikurs suggested that the person who has the most influence on our personality development is not necessarily our mother or father, but the sibling closest to us in age—the one with whom we are most in competition.[31]

"Conflict with a sibling is one of the ways that shapes who you are as a person, because personality really means the style you've adopted to interact with others in the world, and that involves a lot of trial and error early on in life," says Dr. Given.[32]

Changes as Older Siblings Become Adolescents

The many changes that occur as an older sibling enters the teenage years affect the sibling relationship also. There is often lower tolerance of younger siblings' antics, or the older one may assume a more parental role. Now the desire of the younger brother or sister to be with the older sibling becomes bugging. This is hard for younger children to understand, because they admire the older sibling even more as he or she becomes less available or interested in them.

Friend or Foe?

1. You've heard a lot about sibling rivalry. You think sibling rivalry is:
   a. *a completely bad thing.*
   b. *an opportunity for learning.*
   c. *a completely good thing.*

2. You think dealing with brothers and sisters is a lot like dealing with people at work. Your friend asks you why it's similar. You say:
   a. *you didn't choose the people at work.*
   b. *you have to be around each other, so it's easier if you get along.*
   c. *both of the above.*

3. When you have a sister or brother, one of the things you learn is:
   a. *you have to share resources with someone else.*
   b. *you are the only one your parents love.*
   c. *you are better than everyone else.*

4. Parents model conflict resolution for their children. You think this means parents should:
   a. *never argue.*
   b. *not worry about how their fighting affects their kids.*
   c. *settle their arguments by apologizing and reaching a compromise acceptable to both.*

5. Your parents are always ragging on you because your grades aren't as good as your sister's. It makes you really angry. You:
   a. *join the Foreign Legion.*
   b. *tell your parents that it hurts you when they say this.*
   c. *don't let your parents see how you feel.*

6. One of your friends says he read that parents should just let kids fight. You:
   a. *agree and say, "May the strongest win!" because you are bigger than your brother.*
   b. *disagree because your brother is bigger than you are.*
   c. *feel kids sometimes need guidance from parents.*

Answers on Page 110

4

The Teenage Years

"If I don't hear that bathwater running, you're dead!"

That certainly is not the voice of someone in *The Babysitters Club*. It is instead the voice of a fourteen-year-old who has been asked to oversee bathtime for his eight-year-old brother. His method is to shout from the family room where he is comfortably watching TV.

Taking care of younger siblings is just one of the areas where teenagers find themselves with mixed feelings about the sibling relationship. One of the reasons adolescence is a turbulent time is that during this period a normal individual begins the process toward adulthood both physically and emotionally. It is a time of turning inward, of being concerned with his or her own worth, as well as peer relationships. Along with the new thirty-minute daily shower is an interest in romantic relationships. To his family the teenager is saying: "I am me, I'm not just an extension of you anymore!" At the same time, this process of separation can also bring on a deep sense of loss and isolation that feels like grieving.[1] And, of course, there is not a steady, methodical process toward maturity with every teenager, but a series of individual forays and retreats. One day she can want independence from her impossible family so badly she cannot wait one more minute; the next day the thought of leaving, even in the future, moves her to tears.

Arrivals and Departures

Along with personal changes in adolescence, often the structure of the family changes with the arrival of new brothers or sisters (new births or adoptions) and by older siblings leaving (for example, marrying or going away to college).

A new baby coming into the home means parental attention is diverted for a time; perhaps the younger child is moved out of his or her bedroom. Birth order changes as the youngest child now becomes the middle child; or, in the case of adoption of an older child, the oldest could move down a step in the family constellation (birth order). A new baby could be an embarrassment or it could be seen as a substitute baby for the adolescent's self. Older children might now have to share space that was exclusively theirs before. The family has changed, and it takes time for everyone to adjust.

Tom, fifteen, was in his room looking through a sports magazine when his parents knocked on his door, came in, and hesitantly informed him that they were expecting another baby.

"Oh, well," said Tom, nonchalantly flipping over another page, "There goes another $140,000."

Everyone laughed at his quick reply, which showed he had been reading about how much it cost to raise a child to the age of eighteen at that time. However, it was also an acknowledgment by Tom that a new baby would mean a drain on the family finances, not to mention parental time and energy, which would affect him in many ways that were as yet unknown.

An older sibling leaving, even if anticipated, causes change also.

"I don't want this year to end," said eleven-year-old Ross to his father as they were riding in the car one afternoon near the end of May.

"Why?" responded his father. "Are you having such a great time at school?"

"No," said Ross. "It's because I don't want Mark to leave."

Mark was Ross's older brother, who was graduating from high school in June and going away to college in the fall.

On the other hand, Mark's brother Peter, who was turning thirteen, was looking forward to the departure. With Mark gone, Peter would be the oldest sibling at home, enjoying the benefits of that rank.

As Ross expressed, there can be a sense of loss as an older sibling leaves for a new stage in life. Even an eleven-year-old knows that the day-to-day family contact will never be quite the same. Or, as Peter showed, there can be relief at the change.

With all these changes going on, there are bound to be changes in the sibling relationship as well. It may

The Teen Years

Fifty-five high-school students who had older siblings were asked to comment on whether they felt things were better or worse since they themselves started high school. Fifteen said the relationship had improved, eight said things were worse, twenty-one said they were the same, five said things had just changed but could not say if they were better or worse, four said that the relationship had always been good, one said it varied—sometimes good, sometimes bad—and one said it had never been good and he avoided his older sibling.[2]

Lorena, fourteen, says, "Things have changed a lot since I started high school because my older brother gives me more attention than when I was in junior high. We now talk more and get along very well."

Lola, fifteen, finds a lot has changed with her eighteen-year-old sister. "We hang around more with each other and we communicate more."

Sometimes what happens is a pulling back from emotional involvement with each other. Sonia, fourteen, states that she and her seventeen-year-old brother used to fight a lot when they were younger, but now he leaves her alone—and fights with their little brother!

Hilda says that everything is the same because she and her eighteen-year-old sister have always been "best friends."

be better with older siblings and worse with a brother or sister close in age. And, just when other interests are much stronger, a teenager may find himself the often reluctant caregiver for younger siblings.

Older Siblings

Few studies have been done on adolescent sibling relationships, and even in those studies there is disagreement on how the sibling relationship changes during the teenage years.

One expert has commented that teens are ambivalent and have mixed feelings about their relationships with brothers and sisters, but they do rely on them as confidants, especially regarding relationships with friends, use of drugs, sexuality, and other issues that appear during adolescence.[3] This ambivalence makes it hard to find a textbook pattern that describes individual relationships during these years.

One aspect of this relationship is clear: older siblings are strong role models. This can be good, as in the case of Tawni and Phil in an earlier chapter, or the teen who said his older brothers kept him from being in a gang.

However, older siblings who make bad choices can have a very negative impact on younger brothers and sisters. For example, a recent study suggested that if an older teenage sister has a baby, her younger siblings are more at risk of becoming teenage parents themselves.[4] There are many reasons why this might happen. One reason might be that the younger siblings see the family limits of acceptable behavior as now being stretched. Another reason might be that the attention the older sister and her baby get in the beginning seems attractive to younger siblings. Also, if the older sister

Better Times Ahead

A recent research study identified certain characteristics about the way sibling relationships change from childhood into adolescence.

The power and status structure changes as children get older and differences in abilities and status lessen. For example, although the abilities of one-year-old and four-year-old brothers are very different, by the time these siblings are eighteen and twenty-one, they will be fairly balanced in what they are able to do. As this happens, their relationship becomes more like that of peers. As children grow older, their sibling relationships generally become less intense, probably in part because they spend less time together.

Birth order affects how children feel about their experiences with their brothers or sisters. This means that older and younger children often see their relationship differently. An older sibling tends to be more nurturing and dominating while a younger one experiences being cared for and dominated. Later-born siblings report that conflict drops off with age; older siblings did not feel this happening.[6]

remains at home with her baby, life for her younger brothers or sisters becomes much more difficult.

"One thing to make the family aware of is that the younger siblings get overlooked," said Patricia East, of the University of California, San Diego, School of Medicine. "Parents need to look at the very difficult transition that [the younger siblings] are going through and give them and opportunity to talk about it."[5]

Siblings Close in Age

Teens close in age to a brother or sister may find increased areas of conflict. "We don't talk as much as when we were younger," says Laura, fifteen, adding that she and her fourteen-year-old sister also fight more now. Blanca, fifteen, says that her brother, thirteen, "is the total opposite of me, we don't get along at all." Emily, eighteen, finds that what has been hard for her is a role reversal with her twenty-year-old sister: "When we were younger, it was a lot easier because she was who I looked up to, but now she seems to follow my lead."

At times it may be a good thing to be different from a sibling. Dr. Brody says that if teens have different areas in which they excel or that they value in terms of their own identity, then probably they have a better chance of having a closer relationship. "The reason for this," explains Dr. Brody, "is that it allows you to bask in the glory of a brother's or sister's accomplishments and through that association enhance your own self-esteem, rather than having to spend most of your time deciding if you are stacking up as well as your brother or sister in that same dimension."[7]

Caregivers—Relationships with Younger Siblings

With more parents working outside the home, as well as more single-parent families, many teens find themselves assuming a caregiver role in the family. Out of one hundred teenagers questioned, almost half helped take care of younger siblings.[8] They had mixed feelings about this, as expressed by Alicia, fifteen: "I don't like taking care of my little sister because she gets on my nerves and bugs me a lot, but it is also fun because she can be funny."

For many teens, the issue of responsibility is what stands out: "You feel like you have power and that you can help them grow up like they should," says Jimmy, oldest of five. Patty finds that watching younger siblings is a preparation for the realities of parenthood: "You get to learn how much responsibility you will have when you get older."

However, some teens would echo Mick, who has to watch his four younger siblings, sixteen months, two, six, and ten: "Nothing is good—it's a pain in the butt." Tanya's main complaint is that because she has to take care of her three younger siblings, she can't go out.

Experts also have found good and bad in being caretakers for younger siblings. Hanne Sonquist, a marriage and family therapist, says that sometimes older siblings are very good caregivers, but if they have high standards they can be perceived as being bossy or excessively strict. "Also," she adds, "older siblings can be resentful of taking care of younger brothers and sisters if it keeps them from doing other things."[9]

Child psychologist Dr. Paul Meisel feels that taking care of younger kids is a valuable experience, both for the growth in responsibility and for giving teens an appreciation of their parents.[10] Jason, fourteen, who takes care of his two-year-old sister three times a week, says that the good thing is that it gives his mother (a single parent) a break.

There are some basic issues that come up under caregiving, says Dr. Meisel: "First, parents should give the sibling caregiver a situation they can handle and enough authority and education about it. Second, the older child needs to get a good amount of nurturing, because the caregiver role is very demanding. Last, teens need to be able to lead their own lives."

Dr. Meisel offers these suggestions for teens who are struggling with their caregiver roles. "Rather than tell the parent that you don't want to do the job, you might be better off to try to figure out what would be worth it to them for you to do the job. For some kids it's money, for some it's privilege, for some it's the freedom to really do it, and for others it's time alone with the parent. Perhaps the best thing is to ask yourself, 'What would make it worth it, if anything?' and go from there."[11]

Hanne Sonquist adds, "Sometimes when there aren't a lot of options—working parents, not much money—you might have to live with resentment, but don't take it out on your younger siblings. Write your feelings down, talk to your friends."[12]

And as difficult as Tanya and Mick and others in the same position find their roles, these teens possess an enormous power for good or bad over the lives of their younger brothers and sisters. Jacob, sixteen, sums it up: "I don't like losing my own time, but it's good to spend time with my brother and teach him things." Dr. Meisel says that part of the problem is that older siblings see the younger one's attention as bugging, when often it is really hero worship of the older brother or sister.[13] As the younger siblings grow older, the bond formed during these often boring or frustrating days of caregiving can be one that develops into deep and lasting friendship.

Stressful or Violent Sibling Relationships

Studies have shown that sibling violence is the most prevalent form of family violence. One study concluded that violent interactions between siblings, particularly for the one who commits the violence, is more important than any other familial interaction in socializing persons to behave violently. In other words, if there is a bully in the family—one sibling who consistently physically abuses the other siblings—it is likely that he or she will be violent in dealing with those outside the family as well.[14]

Without the intervention of adults, it is difficult for the other siblings to deal with this situation. Sometimes, as in the case of Karl, seventeen, whose older stepbrother was violent and often in trouble with the law, avoidance is the only avenue.

Fighting itself is not the issue, but physical abuse of one sibling or relationships in which one sibling is consistently afraid when the brother or sister walks into the house need to be dealt with. "Sometimes," cautions Dr. Meisel, "the one who's getting harsh treatment tends to be reasonably provocative. So, the one intervening needs to be aware of all that is going on in the abusive interaction."[15]

"However," says Stan Speck, "a younger sibling can think, 'Well, I brought this on. If I didn't make them so angry, they wouldn't treat me like this.'" Speck says often younger siblings are afraid to tell the parents, because then the older sibling will beat them more later on.

If parents do not intervene, sometimes outside help is necessary. However, Speck feels that getting the whole family involved in addressing this issue is important. "I believe families are capable of changing themselves," says Speck, "but counseling as a therapy component can speed things up, and the abused sibling can know that if the brother or sister comes after them again, it's going to be reported."[16]

What Would You Do?

1. **Your ten-year-old sister is always coming into your room and bothering you. You:**
   a. *punch her and scream insults at her.*
   b. *ignore her and hope she'll go away.*
   c. *talk to your parents about making a rule that rooms are off-limits to siblings unless invited. Then give your sister an appointment for a short visit.*

2. **Your sister is totally different from you. Now that you are both teenagers, you:**
   a. *have a good chance to get along better because you aren't competing in the same areas.*
   b. *should try to be more like her.*
   c. *won't get along because you have different interests.*

3. **Your mother is a single parent and needs you to take care of your brother. Some friends invited you to go downtown, but you have to stay home. You:**
   a. *get really mad at your brother.*
   b. *talk to your mother about making the situation better.*
   c. *feel that you are the unluckiest person in the world.*

4. **It bugs you that your younger brother wears the same kind of clothes you do. You:**
   a. *are probably his hero.*
   b. *think he's trying to look better than you.*
   c. *rip them off of him.*

5. **You like to listen to alternative music and your brother is a rapper. He plays his stuff really loud and you can hear it in your bedroom. You:**
   a. *talk to him when you've cooled down.*
   b. *don't say anything but meditate on how selfish he is.*
   c. *sell his stereo system.*

6. **Your older brother is constantly physically abusive. You:**
   a. *tell him if he doesn't stop you will have to get help.*
   b. *go to your parent or a trusted adult for help.*
   c. *do both of the above.*

Answers on Page 110

5

Siblings in Special Circumstances

In some families there are challenging situations that put distinct demands on sibling relationships. These include having a brother or sister with special needs, divorce and one-parent families, stepsiblings, twins, only children, death of a sibling or parent, alcoholic parent or sibling, and sibling incest.

Siblings With Special Needs

In the 1988 movie *Rain Man*, Charlie Babbitt, the character played by Tom Cruise, discovers only as an adult that he has a brother—a brother with special needs. The movie shows how Charlie finally learns to accept his brother for who he is.

There are a lot of issues that affect the way people

react to a sibling with special needs. First is the overall climate in a society. Dr. Susan McHale of the Department of Human Development, Pennsylvania State University, says, "One thing that needs to be kept in mind is that times have changed significantly in terms of how society deals with handicapped and mentally retarded children. They went from being totally institutionalized to mainstreamed in the 1970s and 1980s. Now, the present climate recognizes that mainstreaming at all costs might not benefit special needs children the most, that they do need tailored programs."[1]

Meeting Special Needs. Although fiction, the movie *Rain Man* parallels to some extent the changes that have occurred in this area. In keeping with a former norm in society, Raymond, the autistic brother played by Dustin Hoffman, has been institutionalized and basically removed from the family; in fact, in spite of some shadowy childhood memories, Charlie Babbit does not even know he has a brother. When he is confronted with the existence of Raymond, Charlie is also confronted with weaknesses in himself, and as his level of caring for his brother grows, he wants to make Raymond fit into normal life—his life. Through a series of incidents, Charlie realizes that as much as he loves Raymond, Raymond needs special care that he alone cannot give him. However, both brothers gain from the relationship.

The overall climate of society is one factor that affects how a family deals with the impact of a special needs child. Another factor is the place where the family lives: some areas might have more facilities, such as special schools, available, or the attitude of one community might be more accepting of handicapped or disabled children than another community. Social class seems to make a difference as well, notes Dr. McHale. She says, "For upper-middle-class families, there's one right way to be, so it's much harder to have a special needs child in the family in terms of how that violates the parents' and the family's expectations about achievements." Other factors that affect the sibling relationships in families with a special needs child are how long the parents have been married, what their marriage is like, and the age of the special needs child.

Sibling Role Reversal. There also tends to be a role reversal among children in the family. If the older sibling is mentally disabled, for example, the nondisabled sibling takes over the role of the firstborn. The nondisabled sibling also often feels an added pressure to achieve, even if this is unexpressed by the parents, especially if there are only two children in the family. This sibling often has extra responsibility and can become the parental helper. Like other patterns in families, the way this is handled by the parents can make it either a positive or a negative experience.

The issue of fairness has a special slant. Treating two kids differently does not have the same effect in families with a disabled child as it does in families without. In a family with a special needs child, there is a clear-cut reason why children are treated differently, and the normal sibling understands this. Of course, this doesn't mean that their emotions will fall into line. It's only natural to feel resentful at times and guilty for feeling that way.[2]

Since the 1960s, much research has been done on individuals who have a brother or sister with special needs. Studies have found that siblings tend to share a

Alice

Alice has a mentally disabled younger brother, Ken. Now in her twenties, Alice looks back on her years at home with her brother with some mixed emotions, but also with gratitude for the things Ken has taught her.

While at a Christian college in Chicago, Alice worked in the school's social service outreach program. "It was a lot of fun until I began work in a center for special needs kids," *she later said of the experience.* "Then it really hit home. Seeing all those kids in an institution and thinking, this could have been Ken—it was emotionally challenging. I realized how fortunate we had been that we had been able to keep Ken at home. For many of the kids at the center, their families had no choice: either the handicaps were too great or there just weren't enough resources at home to deal with all the demands of a special needs child."

Alice went on to say, "I think I really appreciated then what my parents had done. It was hard in many ways growing up, especially in my early teen years, but I always had great love for Ken, who is only two years younger than I am. I remember praying as a child, 'Please help the people in Africa get enough food and help my brother learn how to talk.' I think that my parents gave each of us—I have a brother younger than Ken also—individual attention, so that none of us felt ignored. During my childhood, I did talk about my feelings about Ken to my parents, but I didn't tell them that I was embarrassed to bring kids home. After I got to high school, I thought, 'Well, if you don't like my brother, you aren't really a friend.' I developed a take-it-or-leave-it attitude to my friends, which actually made it easier. I also came to accept Ken just for who he is. The worst times were in public, because when Ken gets frustrated, he just has a hissy fit—he pulls hair and gets very physical—and that's embarrassing. I remember one family trip a few years ago when we were at Mount Rushmore and there were just too many people and too much waiting for Ken to tolerate, so he threw a tantrum. There he was, pretty big, acting like a little kid. I just melted away, and when I was out of sight, I looked around and there was my younger brother, Greg—he'd melted away, too! We laugh about it now, even my parents.

"As a family, we've often done certain things because of Ken, which actually have turned out to benefit us all. My parents didn't want a TV, but they got one so that Ken could watch Sesame Street. Now, since nobody else wanted to watch Sesame Street over and over, they've ended up with three TVs!

"I do think about things. Looking at Ken and wondering what he is thinking about, trying to figure out what he wants to say, concern for his future—all these pop up now and then. When I was dating, Ken was a kind of litmus test—if a boyfriend could accept Ken, then that was a real plus. My husband, Mark, had never been in a situation with mentally handicapped kids before he met Ken, but he had an open attitude, and now Ken likes Mark better than he likes me!

"I think one of the main things Ken has taught me is to look at perfection in a different light. We think of it one way, but I have come to believe that God doesn't look at perfection the way we do. We can't begin to comprehend what God has in store for someone like Ken. What Ken achieves on his level can be valued as much as what a normal person does."

number of concerns. These include questions such as "Why does my sister have a disability?" "Why must my parents spend so much time with my brother?" "Why do I have such mixed feelings about my sister?" "What should I do when my friends tease my sister?" "Will my children have a disability—is it genetic?"[3]

"The bottom line," says Dr. McHale, "is communication. It's vital that there be open lines of communication between parents and children so that siblings can talk openly about feelings of resentment without having to worry that parents are going to be hurt or burdened by their point of view."[4]

There is much that is positive about having a sibling with special needs. A study done of college students in 1972 by Frances Grossman found that many of those who grew up having a lot of responsibility for handicapped brothers or sisters were more responsible, were more altruistic, had more social concerns about how the world works, and felt more responsibility for others.[5]

As Dr. McHale says, "Kids with special needs siblings might be paying now for a more mature outlook and stronger character in the long run—not because they had a sheltered and easy childhood, but because they faced challenges."[6]

Divorce and One-Parent Families

In an informal survey of one hundred Santa Barbara High School students with a span of economic, age, and grade levels, forty-three lived with a single parent. Out of the remaining fifty-seven, many of them had been through a parental divorce, and several lived with grandparents.[7] These unofficial figures may be higher or lower in different parts of the country. However, 1,191,000 marriages in the United States ended in divorce in 1994.[8] In 1994, 27 percent of children under the age of eighteen lived with one parent; of these children, 88 percent were with their mothers.[9] There are many teenagers who, in addition to the normal ins and outs of the sibling relationship, have to deal with the effects of parental divorce.

In most cases, the years preceeding the divorce were times of much fighting between the parents. We explored some of the effects of this conflict in Chapter 3. Divorce is not usually an isolated incident but part of an ongoing struggle. Dr. E. Mark Cummings of the University of West Virginia has found that rather than just considering the trauma caused by the divorce itself, it is necessary to look at the level of parental fighting in the period surrounding the separation. Divorce as a means of escape from conflict is not always effective—often conflict increases after the divorce. According to a 1976 study, 66 percent of parental inter-actions after the divorce were angry and hostile. It is well documented that parental fighting predicts chil-dren's aggressiveness and conduct problems during the period of marital dissolution. Problems include depres-sion, withdrawal, inhibition, and anxiety.[10]

Marlene, ten, experienced anxiety over her parents' divorce. "I wish they wouldn't fight," she said. "It makes me feel like it's my fault." At her father's house she felt that he and his second wife favored their own kids over her and her brother Kenny. "Sometimes it doesn't seem there's any place for me," was her conclusion.

In recognition of this need for a place, Suzy Yehl Marta started a support group called Rainbows for children and teens who had experienced a loss through death or divorce. Marta realized that kids needed an opportunity to share feelings with other kids their age who were going through similar upheavals in their family lives.[11]

Effects on Teens. While there seems to be no age group for which divorce is not damaging, the most detrimental effects of family breakup are seen with teenagers. Dr. Judith Wallerstein, founder and former director of the Center for the Family in Transition in Corte Madera, California, found that 68 percent of teenagers engage in some type of illegal and/or self-destructive activity following divorce.[12]

Adolescents in the same family often respond differently to divorce. However, for all involved, divorce is a painful event. Often the pain is too intense for the adolescent to express and he or she finds little recourse. One study found that divorce not only can interfere with the normal developmental stages that a teenager goes through (see Chapter 4) but also can hurry them up. Often they are unable to turn to parents for solace because the parents are going through tremendous emotional upheaval themselves. Adolescents also are forced to see their parents in a different light; often there is a sense of betrayal and anger. Parents may revert to their own preadult behavior, turn to the adolescent for support and comfort, use the adolescent as an unconscious extension of themselves, try to prevent an independent relationship between the young person and the separating parent, or exhibit other disturbing conduct.[13] As Dr. Meisel points out, "When people are divorcing and dealing with divorce, they probably need to be the best version of themselves, but divorce is a place where people feel so bad that they don't have all the resources they need to be that 'best version.'"[14]

Defense Mechanism. Most of the adolescents interviewed in a project at the Community Mental Health Center of Marin County, California, made use of distancing and withdrawal as a defense against experiencing the pain of family disruption. This disturbed the psychologist interviewers, because it seemed that the teens were not sensitive to their families. However, at a later date, these same teenagers were able to be supportive and empathetic toward their parents. It seemed that the youths who appeared able to do best frequently were those who were able at the outset of the divorce to establish some distantce from the parental crisis. In fact, most of the teenagers studied were able within a year following the parental separation to have made an adjustment to their situation and to proceed toward adulthood at a more normal rate. Those who already had problems prior to the divorce seemed to continue to struggle.[15]

Effects on Sibling Relationships. What about the sibling relationship in the face of this severe family trauma? How siblings help each other cope with their parents' divorce, as with other situations, depends on what the relationship was like before.

Steve, now in his thirties, talks about the way that he and his sisters and brother clung together in the face of parental fighting that often turned physically violent and remained destructive after the divorce. He says the knowledge that all the siblings were united gave him the ability to hang on. He credits his older sister, Julie, for imparting to the rest of her siblings the reassurance to be strong and that they would "make it." Steve says, "I really can't imagine what would have happened to me if it hadn't been for her."

Should one sibling go with one parent and the other stay with the remaining parent? Dr. Meisel says, "Even though there are times when it might be appropriate, it is usually a bad thing to separate siblings. It just adds to the loss that they suffer." He adds, "Kids get neglected not out of bad intent but out of lack of judgment and resources. This is one of the reasons to keep siblings together: they have each other."[16]

Kristen, now in her twenties, was just two months old when her parents were divorced. She says she cannot imagine what it would have been like if she had not had her older sister. "She's the only one who knows what it was like, the only one who shares the growing up with a single parent, the visits to our dad, all that."

Stepsiblings

By the end of the century, single-parent and stepfamilies could be a majority in the United States, according to Wendy Geis-Rockwood, a licensed clinical social worker, who teaches classes called "Winning as a Stepfamily." She says the structural differences in stepfamilies that make them different from biological families need to be considered in dealing with the special issues that come up between stepsiblings.[17]

Often stepsiblings are thrown together under the worst circumstances. Sometimes when one parent remarries a person who brings his or her own kids into the family, the mother or father who has not found a new spouse is angry and upset and feeling betrayed. If the kids are caught in the middle, liking their new

Stepfamilies Are Complicated

The following situations create structural differences in stepfamilies and further complicate stepsibling relationships:

1. All individuals have suffered many important losses: relationships, community, dreams about what marriage would be like.

2. All individuals in the family come together with previous family histories.

3. Parent-child relationships predate the new couple relationship.

4. There is a biological parent elsewhere in actuality or in memory with power and influence over family members.

5. Children are members of two households if they have contact with both biological parents.

6. Little if any legal relationship exists between stepparents and stepchildren.[18]

family means betraying one parent; not liking it means betraying the other.

"Just because two adults love each other doesn't mean the kids love this person or their children, but everybody tries to run around and act like it," says Dr. Meisel. "It's better to give kids permission not to love each other, to say, 'Maybe someday, when you've been around a long time with them, you might, but I don't know why you would now—it's just like meeting somebody new.'"[19]

It is also inevitable that competition between stepsiblings will develop as children in the family try to find their places in the system and as children share their biological parents with a stepbrother or sister. "This can be helped," says Geis-Rockwood, "if parents give their biological children the reassurance that they are still as important and provide them an opportunity to ventilate to the parent their resentments about the stepsiblings." Competition arises most often over who gets what—for example, clothes, toys, money, etc. It is best to keep spending roughly an equal amount, but not necessarily in the same way.[20]

Twins and Multiples

"Oh, look. Twins, how adorable!" might be a common reaction as the stroller passes by with two little heads bobbing up and down. For onlookers it might be difficult to see how twins could be regarded as a challenging situation for a family.

However, for the three-year-old brother trailing along listening to such comments, which usually do not include him, it is a different story. It is also a different story for a twelve-year-old sister walking back and forth with two howling babies while her mother tries to get dinner fixed. And perhaps the onlooker might ask a fourteen-year-old what it is like to have two two-year-olds ransack his room and unravel his latest tapes into creative new shapes.

For the twins themselves there are other factors. "Oh, how lucky, they always have someone to play with!" says the bystander. That is certainly true, and

Terri and Harold Craig

Terri and Harold Craig faced the "yours, mine, and ours" situation when they married twenty years ago. Terri had a three- and a four-year-old, and Harold's children from his first marriage were fifteen and seventeen. Together they have five children whose ages today range from eighteen to eight, bringing the grand total to nine children!

Terri says that when she and Harold decided to marry, "the best thing we did was to take it slow." They kept their own relationship in the background and spent lots of time together on weekends with all the kids. "When we went camping, it was girls in one tent and boys in the other—all of us!" she laughs. "We dated for a year and a half, and during that time we all went for counseling, which helped us confront the issues we would be dealing with as we brought two families together."

The issue of discipline was one that she was particularly glad they addressed. They agreed to present a united front and if possible to discuss what they would do ahead of time. She says this really helped when the children from her first marriage turned eleven and twelve and began to argue with Harold about his decisions. "You aren't our real dad. We don't have to do what you say!" the children would say. Harold would respond that he loved them, would always love them, but they had to do what he said. "Mom!" the kids would call, and Terri would say, "Yes, you have to do what he says."

Terri notes that they made sure to do lots of fun things together and to spend as much time as possible with each child. Now she says the relationship between her children and Harold is close-knit—in fact, Craig, the oldest, now twenty-five, works with his stepfather. Terri says that the relationships between the stepsiblings are also close, which she feels was helped greatly by the time they spent allowing for an adjustment period.

for many twins the achievement of one is an achievement for both.

When twins Andrew and Russell were seven years old, they played on the same team in their first soccer game. Andrew scored a goal. As he realized the ball had gone into the net, he turned around and anxiously scanned the field for his brother. When he spotted Russell, he ran toward him. They met midfield and with arms around each other ran over toward their parents. For both of them, Andrew's goal was an achievement shared.

However, the united front often presented to the world can undergo changes as twins approach adolescence. Competition, especially among same-sex twins, can become a major factor in the relationship. Twins seem constantly to be compared to one another, each twin can feel a burden of responsibility for the other, and they may have difficulty in developing a self-concept.[21]

These examples, taken from interviews of twins, illustrate some problems twins face. In one instance, during their early teens, people told Diane and Donna apart because "Donna was the fat twin." Actually, their weights were similar; Donna just looked heavier and neither was fat. Nevertheless, Donna felt like a pig every time they were compared.[22]

Betty and Linda, fourteen-year-old identicals, were both attractive and outgoing. Both tried out for cheerleading at their junior high school but only Betty was chosen. Their mother made Betty reject the position because her twin was not selected. Their parents insisted that they not run against each other in class elections. Since they were not permitted to compete outwardly, they became more and more resentful of each other.[23]

The issue of competition came to a head during their high-school years for identical twins Spencer and Brian, whose parents are divorced. Brian decided to move away from his mother and twin brother to live with his father in another town during his sophomore year of high school. "All my life, we were always 'The Twins,'" said Brian in a newspaper interview. "I wanted to try something new. I wanted to be on my own for a change."

By moving, Brian had the unique experience of playing opposite his brother in a high-school league basketball game. The six-foot-four-inch brothers spent only that year apart, however, reuniting as juniors when Brian returned.

"I guess we needed to be separated to see how we are different," he said. "I don't know. Maybe that's why we get along so much better now, why we aren't as competitive. We love each other a lot and we hang out together. I consider us best friends."[24]

Only Children

Only children often receive very negative input from the world outside the family.

Erin, fifteen, finds that being an only child has definitely affected the way she relates to peers. She feels she does not understand what other people think or feel, so it is hard to get along with other people. She also feels that it is not fair to give more attention to people with brothers and sisters. As she says, "I live with my mom, so it's just the two of us. I have never met my father, and because I have no brothers or sisters I never have anyone to talk to or to lean on when I'm upset. There's never anyone to go outside with to play games. I would give anything to have a brother or sister."

There is reason for Erin to feel isolated. Out of one hundred students questioned, just seven were only children. Besides isolation, only children deal with commonly held views that they are selfish, lonely, and maladjusted. Even psychologists generally seem to feel that only children are at a disadvantage socially.

However, research has indicated that only children are not necessarily more self-centered than children with siblings, and that for every negative aspect of being an only child, there is a positive. Advantages are that only children receive the absolute attention of parents and get along well with older children and adults. Dr. Kevin Leman, author of *The Birth Order Book*, says, "Overall, only children are always more mature. . . . They love having conversations with older people. They are good negotiators in relationships." He says that only children often have multiple children of their own.[25]

Death of a Sibling

"I drove past a store and wanted to scream: 'How can you people be buying groceries? Don't you know my brother is dead?'" Jennifer paused and gave a wry smile as she went on, "Of course, I couldn't expect the world to stop for everyone else because it had for me, but I thought it should."

Two years ago when Jennifer was twenty, her twenty-three-year-old brother, Paul, was killed in a freak accident in Mexico. The family did not learn of his death until two days later. Jennifer and Paul were the only children in the family and, after a brief period when Jennifer was in junior high and "too young" for her brother, they had been very close. When she learned of his death she went numb. She stayed numb for months. In fact, it was not until almost a year later that the full impact of her loss really hit.

View from the Sidelines. Although Jennifer was a young adult, she experienced many of the same things that children do when they lose a sibling. Children who lose a sibling are often kept on the sidelines of family grief. Since they cannot understand fully what the loss means, or they do not express it as an adult would, family members might not be aware of the depth of their feelings. Parents are often so consumed by their own loss that they cannot provide the comfort that children need. And friends and relatives who might allow children to express their feelings often urge them to be strong for their parents' sake. Also, children grieve in different ways, which can make adults angry. They can be deeply sad or angry one minute and go out to play the next. They often act out feelings instead of talking about them.

For adolescents who lose a sibling it is especially difficult, since they are often hampered by a society that ignores death and does not allow time for mourning. More than one person has been advised to get on with his or her life after a few weeks, when in reality there is no way to hurry grieving. A recent study showed one-third to one-half of adolescent siblings still experiencing guilt, confusion, loneliness, anger, and depression almost two years after a brother's or a sister's death. They may react in ways that are socially not as acceptable, converting their sadness and guilt into anger, with which they lash out at everyone.[26]

Jennifer was away at college when she learned of her brother's death. When she walked in the door of her parents' home, she was immediately met by family friends asking her, "Whom should we contact?" Used to helping others, she took on that role, answering the telephone, fielding all the calls to protect her parents. Every time, the caller asked, "How are your parents?" By the third day, Jennifer wanted to cry out: "What about me? How am I doing?" Because she presented an outward calm, everyone thought she was coping. However, she was experiencing not just the loss of a dearly loved brother but the loss of her family. Her parents were no longer the mother and father she knew, and the family structure had undergone a monumental upheaval.

Lessons in Mourning

When asked how children should mourn in the book *Brothers and Sisters: How They Shape Our Lives*, a surviving sibling said: "Don't be afraid to let out everything you feel, even those crazy feelings. If you feel like crying, laughing, or being angry, do it. Just don't hurt anyone. Go ahead and scream and stomp and kick doors if you have to."

Mixed Emotions. Feelings that accompany a sibling's death should not be ignored or repressed. Unattended grief can cause lifelong repercussions and make it difficult to form relationships with others. As Francine Klagsbrun writes, "People who have not been helped to come to terms with the loss of a sibling as children often become anxious and fearful adults, overreacting to illness, needing to be in control and therefore afraid to take risks, frightened of any unknown situation lest they feel as they had once felt in childhood, helpless, confused, and afraid."[27]

For a teen, there can also be feelings of guilt for not spending more time with a sick sibling or for feeling jealous of the attention the sibling receives in death. The absent sibling becomes idealized; his or her things become almost sacred relics, while the surviving sibling's belongings are just "stuff." If there were two children in the family, the remaining sibling may feel greater expectations placed upon him or her; now he or she is the lone repository for parents' hopes. Teens and young adults may also become preoccupied with fears about dying. Jennifer says that now she is very aware of her own mortality. "Gone is the feeling that 'it can never happen to me' because it did happen to me." She also worries about what it will be like if something happens to her parents. If someone is late, she immediately thinks, "That's it, they're dead."

The most long-lasting and damaging loss to an adolescent may be that of a sibling through suicide. Fear, rage, and guilt can be overwhelming—fear that they, too, might give under the pressures that brought their brother or sister to that place, rage that the sibling would do this to them, and guilt over unresolved conflicts or that they were not able to prevent this from occurring.[28]

Support Systems. In her book *Landscape without Gravity: A Memoir of Grief*, Barbara Lazear Ascher writes, "Grieving is like walking. The urge is there, but you need a guiding hand, you need someone to teach you how."[29] For those going through this "landscape without gravity," Jennifer offers some suggestions that have helped her as she still journeys through this difficult place. She joined a support group sponsored by Hospice, which got her through the first months. Even though she was the youngest in the group and only one of two who had lost a sibling, she found it her biggest help. It forced her to think about her brother's death, something she had avoided by keeping busy with school and activities. Although initially she found herself internally critical and angry at other people in the group, eventually she could acknowledge, "My situation isn't worse than anyone else's," and be comforted by "Yes, that's what I'm feeling, too."

A year after Paul's death, Jennifer underwent counseling for about four months, which helped her sort through more feelings.

Jennifer advises friends of the grieving person to talk about the sibling who died and to keep the grieving person talking, also. "It's hard to know what to say, so sometimes people just avoid you or act like nothing has happened, but I wanted to talk about Paul."

Keeping a journal is a great release for grief, as is writing a letter to the person who has died, expressing things you would have liked to tell him or her as well as what he or she meant to you. And, Jennifer says, "Be angry, if that's how you feel. Even if you're angry at God like I was, that's okay. He can take your anger."

Planning ahead for holidays, birthdays, or anniversaries of the sibling's death is vital, Jennifer counsels. "Don't just try to do normal things. Have your strategy already mapped out so that when you get up that day, you have something concrete to do." For the second anniversary of Paul's death, Jennifer talked to her professors at college ahead of time and took three days off school—the period that encompassed the day Paul died and the day they found out. She hiked to a lake, sat beside the water as it gently lapped the shoreline, and reflected about her life with her brother. She wrote in her journal, wrote Paul a letter, and just took time to confront her emotions. It was hard to be alone, but it was healing. "Our society wants instant fixes," she says, "and there just isn't any for grief. My brother will always be a part of my life."

Alcoholic Parent or Sibling

One of the most destructive problems in a family is when one member is an alcohol or substance abuser. When it is the parent, in addition to dealing with the humiliation of seeing a parent drunk, the child often changes roles, becoming, in fact, the responsible member in place of the parent. A sibling who is an abuser can also bring unwanted and often frightening responsibilities to younger brothers or sisters.

Inconsistency. Stan Speck, who counsels troubled adolescents and their families, finds that there are a lot of emotional issues that come up in an alcoholic family system. In the first place, there is a real inconsistency in moods and outlook of the abuser, so the kids never know what the parent is going to be like when he or she comes home. Speck says, "If you grow up used to it, that's a way of life. You don't recognize, 'Now he's had five drinks.' You just think 'By seven or eight o'clock my dad is either tired or grumpy or irritable, or he's asleep,' or something like that." Some parents can become mean and angry; others get really mellow and do not seem to care about anything. Since there is not any consistency, kids can only base whether they get to do something or not on what state the parent is in. This affects the sibling relationship in many ways. Since the parent is unpredictable, there cannot be consistent enforcement of rules, fairness, or handling of conflicts.

Avoidance. Besides inconsistency, another big issue is not dealing with problems. There is a tendency for things to go unresolved, since it is impossible to see things through while intoxicated. This naturally affects sibling disagreements and conflict, since there is more likelihood for bullying or other abuse of a younger or weaker sibling.

Adaptation. There can be a whole list of adaptations a family makes for the substance-abusing parent. There are siblings taking care of other siblings, making dinner, or making lunches for the next day because the parent does not get up. Mom may call in for Dad and say he is really sick today, when really he is hung over. The kids do not want to wake Dad because he gets so grumpy. Everyone in the family ends up playing a part in maintaining that system, making it possible for the abuser to continue.

Perception. "Normally each sibling has a different perspective of where the parent is," says Speck. "What you see in alcoholism or drug abuse is that it's a progressive kind of problem. Usually it gets worse until it gets to a point where the abuser either hits bottom or gets in trouble with the law or something else makes them look at what's happening. If the parent happens to be using alcohol over a period of years, the oldest kid might say it wasn't so bad, the middle kid might see it as worse, and the youngest might perceive the situation as really bad."

A variation on this would be if the parent has been a heavy abuser during the oldest child's life and stops when that child is nine or ten. Then the youngest child would have a very different perspective from his older sibling on the family as a whole.

Additional Issues. When the substance abuser is a sibling, there are additional issues. The sibling who is abusing the substances can be irritable and unreachable or, alternatively, supplying the younger one with drugs. Sometimes the younger brother or sister knows that the older sibling is using drugs but doesn't tell the parents about it. Speck says, "It's just kind of understood that you don't go around ratting on your brother or sister—what's it going to get you? But the fact that they hold on to that knowledge gives them a different role in the family. This has a tremendous impact if something happens to the brother or sister who is abusing the substance."

For example, if the brother or sister has been using drugs and is in an accident in which he or she is seriously injured or killed, then the sibling who has been holding on to the secret feels tremendous guilt. He or she often feels, "I should have told, I should have gotten some help for her."

Speck says that when he counsels siblings in this situation, he asks them to think about how they would feel if their brother or sister got in an accident or overdosed. Then they can look closely at alternatives. "Sometimes," Speck comments, "it's just recognizing that there is a problem and getting validation for that. By talking it over with a counselor, siblings can realize that it's not their problem, it's their older sister's or brother's problem, and siblings don't need to be hooked by this, to cover for the sibling, or to feel guilty for him or her."[30]

Sibling Incest

A situation in which siblings are involved in serious sexual activity with each other usually happens when the family itself is in trouble. As Doctors Stephen Bank and Michael Kahn write in their book *The Sibling Bond*, siblings rarely become sexually embroiled if there is adequate parenting.[31] They state that incest is more likely to occur if there is parental neglect or abandonment. Also, the incest is more likely to have long-term ill effects on sisters than on brothers, and the younger the child when the relationship begins, the less likely he or she is able to understand or escape it. Preadolescent incest is more likely to be seriously confusing or traumatic. The more information children have about sexuality, the better able they are to understand and defend themselves. They need to understand that inappropriate touching is not okay even for a sibling. Open communication between parent and child can help children bring up concerns and can provide protection for them from the possibility of sibling incest.[32]

When sexual abuse by a brother or sister occurs, it is crippling for the whole family. Speck, who has worked with teens in this situation, says, "You'll have parents taking sides over which child they believe. And, if it gets into the court system, which pits brother against sister, family member against family member, it can be very traumatic." As for the future of the sibling relationship in the face of this most devastating of sibling interactions, Speck says it depends on the degree of abuse, the individuals involved, the type of family, and how it is handled. He says that there have been situations in which the abusing sibling recognized it was wrong and was ashamed but handled it in a way that allowed forgiveness and moving on—as well as a way for it to be checked on without anybody feeling offended. Sometimes separation is the only alternative.[33] The long-term effects on the abused sibling need to be monitored as well.

Friend or Fighter?

1. You have a sister who has Down's syndrome. You sometimes feel embarrassed by her behavior. You:
   a. *should be ashamed of yourself.*
   b. *should yell at her.*
   c. *should accept your feelings and try to accept your sister as she is, realizing sometimes she will do things that are embarrassing for you.*

2. You find that you and your brother are divided over your parents' divorce. What might be something positive you could do?
   a. *avoid each other.*
   b. *seek outside help such as a counselor at school.*
   c. *think up new arguments to throw at him.*

3. Your mother just remarried, and now you have a stepbrother almost your same age you hardly know. You:
   a. *take it easy and expect things to take time.*
   b. *refuse to have anything to do with him.*
   c. *tell your mother she shouldn't have done this to you.*

4. You know that your brother, whom you really care about, is taking drugs. You:
   a. *cover for him.*
   b. *talk to a counselor about your options.*
   c. *figure it's his business.*

5. You have an alcoholic parent, whom you are angry at but also care about. You might try:
   a. *talking to a trusted adult about your frustration.*
   b. *joining a support group such as Alateen.*
   c. *both of the above*

6. Your friend's sister died. You don't know what to say when you see her. You:
   a. *give your friend a hug.*
   b. *let your friend talk about how she feels.*
   c. *both of the above.*

Answers on Page 110

6

Developing Good Relationships with Siblings

🗨 Laetitia leaned forward, her face tightening with anger. "My sister took my skirt and didn't even ask, then when she brought it back, she left it crumpled on the floor. She knows I hate that!"

🗨 "My little brother is totally spoiled," volunteered Tracy. "He gets to do whatever he wants."

🗨 José said, "My older brother told me he'd rather give money to a dog than to me."

🗨 "Every time a guy likes me, my sister tries to take him away. She can't even let me have a boyfriend." Sarah's eyes showed the hurt even as she tried to laugh.

These quotes began this book as examples of sibling rivalry and conflict. While it helps to know the reasons behind the negative elements of the sibling relationship, is it possible to do anything about it, and would teens want to change it if they could?

Some of the comments on the next two pages show that teens feel it is the fault of the other sibling that the relationship isn't better; like LaToya, they just want their sisters (or brothers) to shape up. However, others use the word *we* or *us* to indicate that they recognize that they have a role in what is wrong or what needs improving with their brothers or sisters.

Experts have offered some advice for dealing with problems that come up between siblings. One of the most reassuring is that all of the issues represented by the comments on the previous page are common areas of conflict and that things, in almost all cases, will get better as both siblings mature. As Dr. Meisel says, "Hang together, you're going to do better as time goes on. Things happen now that get in the way, but later you will want each other. Think of it as long-term."[1]

Of course, one of the problems is that siblings often do not have a lot of control over how situations are handled, as in the case of José, whose older brother says he would rather give money to a dog, or Karla, who would like her brother to have more responsibility around the house. In an ideal situation, this could be addressed at a family meeting and a more fair distribution of tasks worked out. However, if this is not the case, what then? What about the little sister who is mean and hits you and you are the one who always takes the blame? What about the sister who tries to take your boyfriend? Or what about the one who "borrows" clothes without asking?

A Change for the Better

Fifty-five percent of people in a recent poll said they wished they had better relationships with their siblings.[2] These are some of the changes teens say would improve their sibling relationships:

- *That she wouldn't act like an old lady!*

  —Will, fourteen

- *Humor—my sister, seventeen, gets mad at everything.*

  —Lorena, fourteen

- *I would like my ten-year-old brother to not get so angry on small things.*

  —Gabe, fifteen

- *I would like us to communicate better and for them not to be such rats.*

  —Silvia, fifteen

- *For my sister to be a little more like me.*

  —Lita, fifteen

- *I'd like it if my brother, fourteen, took more responsibility around the house.*

  —Karla, sixteen

- *I'd just like us to start getting along.*

  —Rosanna, sixteen

☐ *To have more love and affection toward each other.*
—Patty, sixteen

☐ *I'd like us not to fight so much.*
—Jason, fourteen

☐ *I'd like them to respect me more.*
—Oliver, fifteen

☐ *That my younger brother wouldn't be so selfish and that the older one would be more fun.*
—Dick, fourteen

☐ *I'd like us not to argue anymore.*
—Rose, fifteen

☐ *I'd like my little brother to stop whining so much.*
—Jacob, sixteen

☐ *My sister needs to shape up.*
—LaToya, fourteen

☐ *I would like to get along better with them.*
—Amber, sixteen

☐ *That we get closer than we are now, so that we can tell each other almost everything.*
—Ronelle, sixteen

The Younger Sibling Who Bugs You

Experts address the bugging issue in several ways. Dr. John Platt, who has spoken to many groups of teens, has developed some practical options. These are based on the concept of control. Dr. Platt says, "Let's use the example of Betty, the one who felt there was no way she could get along with her 'mean' little sister, and that her mother didn't understand. In her case, which is similar to many I deal with, I'd ask her, 'Who's running your life?' and she would probably answer, 'Well, I am.'

"Then," Dr. Platt continues, "I'd get her to look at the scenario—what went on: her little sister walked by, Betty looked at her, the little sister hit Betty, Betty hit her, then Mom came in and Betty got in trouble. Do you see who's running Betty's life in this situation? It's her little sister. She pulled Betty in and Betty's the one who got in trouble."

Dr. Platt then talks about two or three different ways of looking at it. First of all, he would tell Betty, "You have a right, if you want to, to be completely controlled by your younger sister, but if you want to take control of your life and not be sucked in by this and get in trouble with Mom and Dad all the time, there are some options." Dr. Platt would remind Betty that since she is so much older—over twice the age of the six-year-old—she is almost like an aunt to her sister. "Betty doesn't realize that her little sister looks up to her and would like to have her interaction in a positive way, but Betty won't give it to her. What Betty needs to do to take control is to start giving her little sister some positive attention. I'd role-play with Betty to help her learn some skills or even write down on a piece of paper what to say when something happens.

"For example, if the little sister comes up and says,

'You're a fatso,' Betty might try saying, 'I'm sorry you think I'm a fatso, because I'd really like to be your friend.' Or when her sister sticks her foot into Betty's room to see if she'll scream, Betty could say, 'Susie, do you want to come into my room for two minutes or four minutes?' Although Betty might say, 'Oh, my sister won't give in,' I'd ask her to try it. Betty might think about looking at her sister as a little laboratory rat on whom she's going . . . to test a hypothesis and see if it's right or wrong.

"I always tell kids not to take my word for it," Dr. Platt counsels, "but just to see what will happen when they take control of the situation. After all, Betty always has the option of continuing to let her little sister run her life, and that's okay if that's the way she wants it."[3]

Toe-to-Toe with Close-in-Age Siblings

You may have had the experience while using a computer of accidentally giving a wrong command and having the whole program freeze. No matter what you did, nothing would move. In relationships, too, especially with a sibling close in age, there can be places where everything seems frozen. There are several stategies that can help get a person past those "frozen" places with siblings close in age. These strategies are really negotiating tools.

Negotiation. One of these negotiating tools is to take a problem that seems to come up all the time—such as borrowing clothes without asking—and brainstorm to try to find a solution. Brainstorming is used in business meetings as a way to come up with creative ideas. The way it works is each person writes down as many ideas as possible that might work to resolve the problem. Then each idea is presented and

Practice the Fine Art of Negotiation

1. Make a list of the six areas in which you and your brother or sister have the most trouble. Rate them as to which are most important to you: ***very important, **important, *whatever.

   Example:
   a. **Borrowing clothes**   ★★★
   b. **TV shows**   ★★

2. Show the list to your brother or sister and ask him or her to add anything that he or she feels should be included.

3. Each of you make a solutions list and pick out the best ones to try. Remember to include several options, exchanges, and "I cut, you choose" strategies where each would work best. (Don't worry if some of your solutions sound a bit silly.) Here's an example:

Problem
You want to watch different TV shows.

Solution
1. **Pick a different show you both like.**
2. **Take turns each week.**
3. **Channel-surf both shows.**

the good points or drawbacks listed. No put-downs are allowed! Both parties agree on the idea that has the most good points.

Surprise. Another tool to use in a confrontation is the unexpected. When your brother comes in and changes the television to another channel, he will be expecting you to scream, "Don't touch that television!" So instead say, "I really appreciated your changing the channel. I was getting so tired of the one I was watching."[4]

Doctors Carol and Jeffrey Rubin, in their book *When Families Fight: How to Handle Conflict with Those You Love,* advise starting with easy issues—issues about which you and your brother or sister might disagree but neither feels too strongly. Then when you come up against a real confrontation, you might try one of the following negotiation tools:[5]

1. *Increase the number of options.* If you are certain neither one is going to back down, try to find one more option that can be offered to turn the stalemate into a reasonable solution. For example, there is a party that you and your sister want to go to, but one of you has to baby-sit your niece. You could increase your options by pooling your money to hire an acceptable baby-sitter in your place, or you could trade baby-sitting duties with a friend.

2. *Exchange favors.* This is the basic "I do something for you, you do something for me" idea. "I'll baby-sit for you this time, you do it for me next time" might solve a dilemma if acceptable to both parties. A variation on this might involve yielding on certain issues about which you don't feel too strongly. Maybe your brother wants to go to a movie but does not want to go alone. You are not in the mood to go to a movie, but you do not care that strongly about it. You say okay

Test Your Communication Skills

1. Both you and your brother or sister pick one of the problems you've listed on page 82 as an area where there is disagreement.

2. You present your brother's (or sister's) viewpoint and they present yours. Try to really see the issue through your sibling's eyes.

3. Each write down what you heard. Compare notes.

4. Write down what things are needs and feelings and what are positions. (Remember: expressing needs and feelings gives room to maneuver; taking a position locks us in.)

Needs and Feelings
I really want to watch this show.

Position
I am watching this show.

so he will have someone to go with. Sometimes you both might have to give up part of what you want in the exchange of favors. For example, Pat wants to take the car to the dance and Chip wants it to go to work. There is only one car and both brothers feel strongly. Their compromise: Pat drops Chip off at work and goes to the dance after, but Pat knows that he will have to be available to pick Chip up again. Chip agrees, but he is not totally happy because he won't have the car so that he can leave work right away; he will have to wait for Pat. Both sides have had to give up a little.

3. *"I cut, you choose."* This means there is a certain amount of something available and you need to figure out how to divide it. Joe proposes five video games, his brother Sam chooses which one they will play.

Heading Off Conflict At the Pass

Experts dealing with teens suggest that some problems could be alleviated or stopped from creating lifelong resentments through better communication. In order to deal with problem areas, you must understand your own needs and those of the sister or brother with whom you negotiate. Communication is how we get these needs across. Many times we do not say clearly what we feel or need, or we do not really listen to the feelings and needs of others.

Communication As a Tool. As an illustration of the use of communication to solve a problem, let us look at the situation of Sarah, sixteen, the teen quoted in the very beginning of this book and again at the beginning of this chapter. Sarah had difficulties with her fifteen-year-old sister, Lucy, over guys, even though they were close in other areas. Sarah said, "Every time a guy likes me, my sister tries to take him away. She can't even let me have a boyfriend." The counselor suggested that there were two possibilities: 1) Rather than any real interest in the guys, Sarah's sister wanted more of her attention; or 2) Lucy could be deliberately upstaging Sarah whenever boys are around.

Whatever Lucy's motives, the counselor said it was time for the two sisters to talk since the justifiable resentment Sarah felt over her sister's behavior would lead to more problems if kept inside. However, rather than attack her sister verbally, Sarah should express her feelings about Lucy's behavior in a way that would allow Lucy to feel okay about herself rather than judged or blamed, at the same time reassuring Lucy that she is a pretty great sister overall. There would probably still be competition between the two sisters, but open communication about problems, combined with reassurance about the love they have for each other, would strengthen their relationship when issues develop that could undermine it.[6]

Know When to Walk Away

Sometimes, in a confrontation with a sibling, neither negotiation nor communication seems to work. When this happens and you find yourself ready to tear that brother or sister limb from limb, Dr. Megan Goodwin of Central Michigan University suggests ways to counter your first impulse. She says that one possibility is to come up with some mechanism for yourself that allows you to delay responding. The mechanism might be counting to ten, taking a deep breath, or some other physical activity to relieve the immediate instinctive reaction. Another strategy is to

Communication Breakdown

The policy of open communication is a good one for many areas of dissension. It might help to look at three main areas where communication can break down: first, through just plain ignorance; second, if one side takes a position instead of expressing needs or feelings; and third, when words are used destructively.[7]

1. *Ignorance.* Although often siblings do seem to do things just to be irritating, it is possible that the offending brother or sister does not realize that he or she has really hurt the other. For example, in the case of Laetitia, whose sister had "borrowed" her skirt without asking and left it crumpled, her sister Sandra found out later that Laetitia had been upset. Sandra said, "I didn't know she felt like that. I was in a hurry that day and I should have asked, but I didn't think she cared."

2. *Taking a position vs. expressing needs and feelings.* Talk about your needs and feelings, don't just take a position. Taking a position traps you into a no-retreat situation. Rather than saying, "The TV is mine tonight," try "I really have been looking forward to watching ESPN tonight; could we work something out?"

3. *Destructive vs. constructive comments.* You should be honest about how you feel, but not destructive. For example, telling your brother, "I feel you should know Bill said you are a real jerk" might be honest, but it is not constructive toward building a good relationship with your brother.

walk away from the conflict until you feel more under control. This is not backing down or chickening out, it is just giving yourself some space before you deal with it—and you do need to come back to it and work it out, not just ignore it. As a third possibility, Dr. Goodwin suggests using other people as resources. This does not mean ratting on your brother or sister, but seeking out someone older who is trusted, either a parent or older sibling or school counselor or some other adult who can help you look at the situation from an outside perspective. Sometimes a peer can be helpful, but often a friend is too close to the situation.[8]

The Warming Effect

Negotiation and communication are just two parts to developing a good relationship, say Doctors Carol and Jeffrey Rubin. The third component is to create good feelings separate from solving disagreements.[9] We might call these engineered good times "warm spots" in our interaction with our brothers and sisters.

There are several ways to create warm spots. It might be helpful to write down some of the things you have done with your sibling that have been fun. By looking at what was happening when things went well, you can see what might be good to try again or even just to talk about together. It can also be beneficial to know what has worked for others. With this in mind, several teens came up with ideas that have been positive in their own sibling relationships. What they found was that often the best times were when they just got away from everyone else. Patty, sixteen, says that she and her sister try to go somewhere by themselves. Emily, eighteen, has good memories of

Shared Time Creates Bonds

For some siblings, family vacations have provided special opportunities to grow closer:

⬜ *My favorite times with my sister are when we go on family vacations together. We can talk along the way. We can also share the same fun things.*

—Caroline, fifteen

⬜ *When we went snowboarding in Colorado, we got along really well and had lots of fun.*

—Jon, sixteen

⬜ *My favorite time was going to Mexico with my brother and sisters.*

—Joe, fifteen

For others, sharing an activity or interest developed ties:

⬜ *The best times are when we go do what we both love—like motorcycle riding and skiing.*

—Buddy, fourteen

⬜ *One of our best times was when we played football in the street.*

—Ericka, fifteen

⬜ *My favorite times are when we're surfing together.*

—Ryan, fifteen

⬜ *When we play Nintendo together—those are the times I like.*

—Greg, fifteen

such moments: "Most of my favorite times were when I was younger, just riding around, me and my sister, no worries and no fights."

A way to improve relationships with younger siblings might include showing them how to do something. Sam, fifteen, helps his younger brothers with sports, and Jed, fourteen, taught his sister to skateboard. Younger siblings enjoyed being treated as equals by their older brothers or sisters.

Just Hanging Out

For many siblings, a favorite thing to do was just spending time together—not doing anything organized.

❏ *It's good just hanging out at home alone with each other.*
—Joe, fifteen

❏ *My best times are when my brothers and I laugh and play around and throw playful insults at each other.*
—Kellie, fifteen

❏ *I like that we are getting to go to high school with each other.*
—Alec, fifteen

❏ *Hanging out together and doing some activities together has helped me with my younger brother.*
—Gunter, fifteen

Even if you followed every piece of expert advice as well as the suggestions above, there are still going to be areas of conflict, hurt, and, yes, even if unexpressed—rivalry. If you asked each of the individuals who commented earlier if they always get along, they would probably say no. What has been given in these examples are suggestions for creating warm spots in the relationship, good times together that will see siblings through the rough places.

Stephi was a teen who used an imaginative approach to create a warm spot in her interaction with younger siblings. Helping her two younger brothers and her little sister to color eggs for Easter gave her the idea for a family egg contest. Everyone contributed a decorated egg (even the parents and a visiting grandmother). Stephi had everyone leave the room while she decided on the awards. The one most anxious about the contest was her four-year-old brother, Ryan, who was worried that his older siblings would win the prize since their eggs were so much fancier. Stephi called everyone back into the kitchen. Ryan ran right to his egg and saw that it had been awarded a prize. Excitedly, he held it up to his mother to read, then, with a mixture of awe and pride in his voice, he told his father, "I won, I won! I won Best Coloring!"

What Stephi had done was to give each egg an award. Ryan's older brother won for Most Detailed Egg. Their mother, who was pregnant, won for Best Decorated Egg by an Expectant Mom. Ryan was too little to realize what his sister had been up to, he just knew he had won! By using humor, compassion, and a little imagination and time, Stephi had done something special not only for Ryan and all her siblings but for her feelings about them as well. She had given them positive affirmation, and in this case if Dr. Platt had asked her "Who's in control?" Stephi could truly have answered, "I am."

What if you try to create some warm spots in your relationship with your brothers and sisters and it seems that it is not working? Dr. Goodwin's advice is that strategies take time to work; what you try might not work the first time, but try again.[10]

As a teen moves through adolescence, so many changes are going on inside that it is often hard to be patient with what is going on outside—that younger brother's loud stereo, that sister's giggly girlfriend who is always over. Dr. Platt said that you can make a plus out of impatience. When you start to get angry, do something right away, remove yourself, count to ten, or whatever it takes. If you know you have a short fuse, you just need to act in a positive way before something builds up. Once again, it is an issue of whether you control the situation or someone else does.[11]

Practice for Parenting

One of the reasons it is important to try to understand the causes of sibling conflict and rivalry is that a lot of the emotions that persist into adult life, affecting our relationships with others, our marriages, and especially the way we interact with our own children, come out of the experiences we have had with siblings. Almost all of the strategies suggested by experts and by teens are also useful parenting skills. Practicing them with siblings helps give you ways to deal with your own children.

A group of high-school students had been dis-cussing their siblings when the talk naturally turned to what they planned to do about their own children. Nick, seventeen, brought up the responsibility involved but said he was looking forward to raising his own kids. Patty, fifteen, who is one of several children, said, "Well, have one and see what happens! You're not going to love it after it turns one or two; you're going to hate it and then you're going to say, 'Patty, please take it away!'"

Everyone laughed, but Patty had brought up some-thing that often is not considered when everyone is oohing and aahing over a cute little baby: Parenting is a tough job. This job is complicated when you are the main resource for more than one child. You are going to need help to create a good environment for your children and sometimes just to make it through the day. You might use the things you liked about the way your parents raised you, take classes, participate in parent-child workshops, and read books.

Many of the areas discussed in this book can be used when dealing with your own children. Strategies such as taking control of a situation, offering limited choices, developing habits to delay response when under stress, and using others as resources are all invaluable tools that can help you with your own par-enting. Finding ways to create warm spots, spending time with each child, being fair, avoiding compar-isons, helping children learn to resolve conflicts, enjoying your role as a mother or father—all these positive strategies will make it rewarding to be a par-ent. They will also make it more likely that your children will be siblings who are friends as well as brothers and sisters.

Create Warm Spots With Your Siblings

1. Make a schedule with your brother or sister to do something fun. Pick out one afternoon a week to try for a month. Choose an activity that you both will enjoy. If you have trouble deciding, do some brainstorming. Pick several activities and list good points and drawbacks for each one. Be careful not to say anything is bad in itself, just stick to drawbacks.

Activity	Good Points	Drawbacks
Play football	cheap lots of action both like it	it's really cold out
Go to the show	both like it inside (cold outside)	costs money
Go in-line skating	lots of action	only one likes it it's really cold out

2. Each of you write down five things you see as the other's strengths. If you want, put each statement on a separate piece of paper and put all five in a brown paper bag as a present for each other.

   Example: Mary is very generous.

Difficult Situations

What if your parents did not create the kind of family atmosphere in which brothers and sisters were able to develop a good relationship? What if you have felt that things were grossly unfair or that your parent or parents favored your brother or sister or did not help you learn to settle disputes in a constructive manner?

Debbie's parents never interfered when Debbie's older brother beat up on her or did mean things to her. She came to fear and hate him—even as an adult, her negative feelings were very strong. She avoided her brother, who still seemed capable of hurting her. Jason's mother bought elaborate presents for his older brother Walter and nothing for him. Patti Mae's father was an alcoholic who was abusive to both her and her brother, but he made it clear that her brother was the favorite child. Grace and her sister had never gotten along. It was only when they were both older adults that Grace realized many of their problems had been caused by their mother's pitting one against the other. When Grace approached her sister with the desire to make peace, her sister responded eagerly and they were able to enter into the relationship they had been cheated of for years. These are just a few instances of poor sibling relationship situations continuing into adulthood that have root causes in parental failure or neglect.

If you are in a similar situation, is there any hope of change? Well, you cannot undo the past, but you can do something about the future if you really want to—and if you do not want to wait like Grace and her sister until you are in your sixties! There are two main possibilities. One is that your parents or your siblings would like to change things, too. If that is the case, you can talk to them about some of the ideas suggested already. Most likely, family counseling is in order.

The second possibility is that your parents or siblings are unable or unwilling to change. If this second scenario is your situation, there are still things you can do to stem the damage caused to yourself. The main—and perhaps only—avenue for you in this case, experts advise, is to get outside help. A trusted adult such as a priest, minister, rabbi, counselor, or teacher at your school could be a resource with whom you could share your struggles and by whom you could be steered toward a place that might offer you more help.

If you have an alcoholic parent or sibling or you are struggling with problems caused by your parents' divorce or a family death, there are wonderful support groups such as Alateen, Rainbows, or Hospice. Support groups are places where you do not have to pretend that things are great; others are there who share your worries or fears and can provide constructive ways for you to deal with them. If you are being sexually or physically abused by a sibling, you could call the National Child Abuse Hotline to find out where to get help. (See *Where to Get Help* at the end of this chapter for the phone numbers of these organizations.)

By getting help yourself through any or several of these means, you will be able to develop into the person you are meant to be, and you also will be better equipped to help your family. You will be able to understand and forgive some of the actions of your parent or sibling without bearing the burden of that person's poor choices. A list of agencies that offer assistance is included at the back of this book.

An Investment for a Lifetime

Perhaps you have never thought very much about the effects that you and your siblings have on each other. The internal background to our sibling relationships is different for everyone. Some of us are firstborn, some are from large families, small families, or different cultural and economic situations. Issues that were big in childhood, such as sharing a room or wanting the same toys, won't be issues later, but the underlying emotions will still be there. In some cases our parents handled the areas of fairness, comparison, and disputes in such a way that they did not produce feelings of bitterness or resentment among siblings. Sometimes, for one reason or another, things were not handled so well. For some of us, special circumstances have made us feel differently about our brothers and sisters than we would have if these had not existed.

In whatever place we are with siblings now, it is worth it to try to make it better. Even though we may never come to the place where there are no disagreements or conflict, we should treat our siblings as highly important parts of our lives. An effort should be made to improve a relationship while recognizing that sometimes it will fail. The bottom line is to persevere, because it says to our siblings, "I care about you, I care about our family. No matter what, I won't give up because this is so important to the future of all of us."

The Hughes twins spoke about being there for each other. A high-school student called it "having backup." One expert said it was something to nurture. Another expert talked about siblings sharing the same memory bank. What can this resource mean to you in the future?

I got a call about midnight three years ago that my parents had been in a car accident and that my mother was critically injured and not expected to live. I drove for three hours to get to the hospital, not knowing what I would find when I arrived. As I entered the emergency room, the first person I saw was my sister; the next one, my brother. The relief I felt was so great it had a physical impact, almost as if I had received a life-giving dose of oxygen. And, even before I knew how our mother was, I was emotionally upheld just by their presence. They knew exactly how I felt—I was not alone. Within hours my other two brothers had arrived. The five of us continued to support each other and my father as we spent long hours together in the intensive care waiting room. We found ourselves often reminiscing and laughing together over incidents in our growing-up years, even in the midst of anxiety over our mother. My siblings and I share the same memory bank.

What we were doing was making a withdrawal from our joint account of memories to cushion us in a time of crisis. You are creating this memory bank with your own brothers and sisters, which will be a resource for you in difficult times. It will also be with you in times of celebration, as it was for me and my siblings as we added to our account the joyous memory of our mother coming home from the hospital on the way to recovery. Your relationship with your brother or sister is one of the longest relationships you will ever have. Your investment in each other, if you make it a good one, will have a lifetime payoff.

Where to Find Help

Alateen or Al-Anon may be listed in your local telephone directory, or contact: Alateen, Al-Anon Family Group Headquarters, Inc., 1600 Corporate Landing Parkway, Virginia Beach, VA 23454. Phone: (804) 563-1600.

Dougy Center, The National Center for Grieving Children and Families, National Directory of Children's Grief Services, 3909 S.E. 52nd Avenue, P.O. Box 86852, Portland, OR 97286. Phone: (503) 775-5683. (Refers you to local agency.)

Hospice Association of America, 228 Seventh St. S.E., Washington, D.C. 20003. National Directory, (202) 547-7424.

National Child Abuse Hotline, 1-800-422-4453.

National Runaway Switchboard, 1-800-621-4000. (Can refer you to local agencies.)

Rainbows, 1111 Tower Road, Schaumburg, IL 60173. Phone: (708) 310-1880, or 1-800-266-3206 (USA and Canada). (Help for children or teens dealing with grief over a death or parental divorce.)

Sibling Information Network, The A.J. Pappanikou Center on Special Education and Rehabilitation, 249 Glenbrook Road, Box U-64, Storrs, CT 06269. Phone: (860) 486-4985. (Serves as bridge for sharing ideas, programs, research, or needs regarding siblings and families of persons with disabilities.)

Stepfamily Association of America, Inc., 215 Centennial Mall South, Suite 212, Lincoln, NE 68508-1834. Phone: 1-800-735-0329.

Chapter Notes

Chapter 1

1. Personal interview with Dr. Gene Brody, research professor, Department of Child and Family Development, University of Georgia, Athens, Georgia, May 22, 1995.

2. Personal interview with Dr. Dean Given, clinical psychologist, Santa Barbara, California, March 23, 1995.

3. Veronica Chambers, "Albert and Allen Hughes: Twins Making Films," *Essence*, July 1993, p. 44.

4. Personal interview with Dr. Paul Meisel, clinical child psychologist, Santa Barbara, California, April 24, 1995.

5. Questionnaire information obtained from students at Santa Barbara High School, Santa Barbara, California, March 15, 1995.

6. Judith S. Brook, Ed.D., Martin Whiteman, Ph.D., David W. Brook, M.D., and Ann Scovell Gordon, M.A., "Sibling Influences on Adolescent Drug Use: Older Brothers on Younger Brothers," *Journal of the American Academy of Child and Adolescent Psychiatry*, vol. 30, November 1991, p. 965.

7. John Zant, "For the Love of Phil," *Santa Barbara News-Press*, March 18, 1995, p. A1.

8. Brody interview.

9. Personal interview with Hanne Sonquist, marriage, family and child therapist, Santa Barbara, California, March 13, 1995.

Chapter 2

1. Personal interview with Dr. Dean Given, clinical psychologist, Santa Barbara, California, March 23, 1995.

2. Dr. Kevin Leman, *The Birth Order Book: Why You Are the Way You Are* (Ada, Mich.: Fleming H. Revell Company, 1985), pp. 10–11.

3. Thomas H. Powell and Peggy Ahrenhold Gallagher, *Brothers and Sisters: A Special Part of Exceptional Families* (Baltimore: Paul H. Brookes Publishing Company, 1993), p. 19.

4. Ibid., p. 29.

5. Leman, p. 154.

6. Personal interview with Hanne Sonquist, marriage, family and child therapist, Santa Barbara, California, March 13, 1995.

7. Powell and Gallagher, p. 29.

8. Sonquist interview.

9. Personal interview with Dr. Paul Meisel, clinical child psychologist, Santa Barbara, California, April 24, 1995.

10. Stephen P. Bank and Michael D. Kahn, *The Sibling Bond* (New York: Basic Books, 1982), p. 10.

11. Ibid.

12. Sonquist interview.

13. Laura M. Markowitz, "Sibling Connections," *Utne Reader*, May/June 1994, p. 57.

14. Personal interview with Tabin Cosio, Santa Barbara, California, May 30, 1995.

15. Meisel interview.

16. Personal interview with Stan Speck, counseling center manager, Klein Bottle Youth Programs, Santa Barbara, California, May 11, 1995.

17. Ibid.

18. Given interview.

19. Personal interview with Dr. Shirley McGuire, assistant professor, Department of Psychology, University of California at San Diego, La Jolla, California, May 1, 1995.

20. Ibid.

Chapter 3

1. Personal interview with Dr. Dean Given, clinical psychologist, Santa Barbara, California, March 23, 1995.

2. Personal interview with Dr. Paul Meisel, clinical child psychologist, Santa Barbara, California, April 24, 1995.

3. Ibid.

4. Personal interview with Dr. Shirley McGuire, assistant professor, Department of Psychology, University of California at San Diego, La Jolla, California, May 1, 1995.

5. Meisel interview.

6. Given interview.

7. McGuire interview.

8. Personal interview with Dr. Megan P. Goodwin, associate professor, Individual and Family Studies, Central Michigan University, Mt. Pleasant, Michigan, April 13, 1995.

9. Meisel interview.

10. Goodwin interview.

11. Personal interview with Dr. E. Mark Cummings, professor, Department of Psychology, West Virginia University, Morgantown, West Virginia, June 16, 1995.

12. E. Mark Cummings and Patrick Davies, *Children and Marital Conflict: The Impact of Family Dispute and Resolution* (New York: The Guilford Press, 1994), p. 144.

13. Ibid., p. 145.

14. Judith R. Brown, Ph.D., *"I Only Want What's Best for You": A Parent's Guide to Raising Emotionally Healthy Children* (New York: St. Martin's Press, 1986), pp. 109–110.

15. Personal interview with Dr. Gene Brody, research professor, Department of Child and Family Development, University of Georgia, Athens, Georgia, May 22, 1995.

16. Meisel interview.

17. Thomas H. Powell and Peggy Ahrenhold Gallagher, *Brothers and Sisters: A Special Part of Exceptional Families* (Baltimore: Paul H. Brookes Publishing Company, 1993), p. 31.

18. Brody interview.

19. Cummings and Davies, p. 97.

20. Personal interview with Hanne Sonquist, marriage, family and child therapist, Santa Barbara, California, March 13, 1995.

21. McGuire interview.

22. Ibid.

23. Powell and Gallagher, p. 151.

24. McGuire interview.

25. Stephen P. Bank and Michael D. Kahn, *The Sibling Bond* (New York: Basic Books, 1982), p. 102.

26. Personal interview with Dr. John M. Platt, M.F.C.C., Elk Grove, California, September 8, 1995.

27. Goodwin interview.

28. Meisel interview.

29. Ibid.

30. Gene H. Brody, Zolinda Stoneman, and J. Kelly McCoy, "Forecasting Sibling Relationships in Early Adolescence from Child Temperaments and Family Processes in Middle Childhood," *Child Development*, vol. 65, June 1994, p. 772.

31. Dr. John M. Platt, Ed.D., *Life in the Family Zoo* (Roseville, Calif.: Dynamic Training and Seminars, Inc., 1991), p. 39.

32. Given interview.

Chapter 4

1. Judith S. Wallerstein, M.S.W., and Joan Berlin Kelly, Ph.D., "The Effects of Parental Divorce: The Adolescent Experience," *The Child in His Family: Children at Psychiatric Risk* (New York: John Wiley & Sons, 1974), p. 483.

2. Information from questionnaire completed by students, Santa Barbara High School, Santa Barbara, California, March 15, 1995.

3. Thomas H. Powell and Peggy Ahrenhold Gallagher, *Brothers and Sisters: A Special Part of Exceptional Families* (Baltimore: Paul H. Brookes Publishing Company, 1993), p. 16.

4. Shari Roan, "The Path of No Return," *Los Angeles Times*, October 21, 1996, p. E1.

5. Ibid., p. E6.

6. Duane Buhrmester and Wyndol Furman, "Perceptions of Sibling Relationships during Middle Childhood and Adolescence," *Child Development*, vol. 61, 1990, pp. 1395–1396.

7. Personal interview with Dr. Gene Brody, research professor, Department of Child and Family Development, University of Georgia, Athens, Georgia, May 22, 1995.

8. Questionnaire.

9. Personal interview with Hanne Sonquist, marriage, family and child therapist, Santa Barbara, California, March 13, 1995.

10. Personal interview with Dr. Paul Meisel, clinical child psychologist, Santa Barbara, California, April 24, 1995.

11. Ibid.

12. Sonquist interview.

13. Meisel interview.

14. Dr. Megan P. Goodwin and Bruce Roscoe, "Sibling Violence and Antagonistic Interactions Among Middle Adolescents," *Adolescence*, vol. xxv, no. 98, Summer 1990, p. 454.

15. Meisel interview.

16. Personal interview with Stan Speck, counseling center manager, Klein Bottle Youth Programs, Santa Barbara, California, May 11, 1995.

Chapter 5

1. Personal interview with Dr. Susan McHale, professor of human development, Department of Human Development, Pennsylvania State University, University Park, Pennsylvania, May 1, 1995.

2. Ibid.

3. Thomas H. Powell and Peggy Ahrenhold Gallagher, *Brothers and Sisters: A Special Part of Exceptional Families* (Baltimore: Paul H. Brookes Publishing Company, 1993), pp. 71–78.

4. McHale interview.

5. Frances K. Grossman, *Brothers and Sisters of Retarded Children: An Exploratory Study*, as described by Powell and Gallagher.

6. McHale interview.

7. Information from questionnaire completed by students, Santa Barbara High School, Santa Barbara, California, March 15, 1995.

8. "Births, Marriages, Divorces and Deaths for 1994" *National Center for Health Statistics Annual Summary* (Hyattsville, Md., 1995).

9. Marital Status and Living Arrangements; Current Population Reports, March 1994, pp. 20–484 (Washington, D.C.: U.S. Bureau of Census), p. A6

10. E. Mark Cummings and Patrick Davies, *Children and Marital Conflict: The Impact of Family Dispute and Resolution* (NewYork: The Guilford Press, 1994), pp. 9–10.

11. Judi Dash, "Healing the Hurt," *Family Circle*, vol. 108, August 8, 1995, p. 19.

12. "How Divorce Affects Children," *Family Circle*, August 9, 1988, p. 86; reprint available from Rainbows, 1111 Tower Rd., Schaumberg, Ill. 60173.

13. Judith S. Wallerstein, M.S.W., and Joan Berlin Kelly, Ph.D., "The Effects of Parental Divorce: The Adolescent Experience," *The Child in His Family: Children at Psychiatric Risk*, vol. 3 (New York: John Wiley & Sons, 1974), pp. 484–485.

14. Personal interview with Dr. Paul Meisel, clinical child psychologist, Santa Barbara, California, April 24, 1995.

15. Wallerstein and Kelly, pp. 495, 503–504.

16. Meisel interview.

17. Wendy Geis-Rockwood, L.C.S.W., "Winning as a Stepfamily," Santa Barbara City College Adult Education class, Santa Barbara, California, October 2, 1995.

18. Cecile Currier, from *Learning to Step Together: A Course for Stepfamily Adults* (Lincoln, Neb.: Stepfamily Association of America, 1982), p. 123.

19. Meisel interview.

20. Geis-Rockwood class.

21. Susan G. Hauser, "Do They Have a 2-for-1 Break on Membership?" *Los Angeles Times*, July 4, 1995, p. E1.

22. Dr. Judy W. Hagedorn and Dr. Janet W. Kizziar, *Gemini: The Psychology and Phenomena of Twins* (Droke House/Hallux, 1974), p. 89.

23. Ibid., p. 92.

24. Dan Shiells, "Year of Separation Brings Teen Twins Closer Together," *Santa Barbara News-Press*, February 5, 1995, p. C1.

25. Dr. Kevin Leman, quoted in "Ties That Bind," by Rebecca Howard, *Los Angeles Times*, February 15, 1995, p. E3.

26. Jane Mersky Leder, *Brothers and Sisters: How They Shape Our Lives* (New York: St. Martin's Press, 1991), pp. 163, 168, 170–171.

27. Francine Klagsbrun, *Mixed Feelings: Love, Hate, Rivalry, and Reconciliation Among Brothers and Sisters* (New York: Bantam Books, 1992), pp. 246–247.

28. Ibid., pp. 248–249.

29. Barbara Lazear Ascher, *Landscape without Gravity: A Memoir of Grief* (New York: Penguin Books, 1994), p. 3.

30. Personal interview with Stan Speck, counseling center manager, Klein Bottle Youth Programs, Santa Barbara, California, May 11, 1995.

31. Stephen P. Bank and Michael D. Kahn, *The Sibling Bond* (New York: Basic Books, 1982), p. 176.

32. Ibid., pp. 195–196.

33. Speck interview.

Chapter 6

1. Personal interview with Dr. Paul Meisel, clinical child psychologist, Santa Barbara, California, April 24, 1995.

2. Joyce Caruso, "Family Ties," *Mademoiselle*, January 1994, p. 90.

3. Personal interview with Dr. John M. Platt, M.F.C.C., Elk Grove, California, September 8, 1995.

4. Ibid.

5. Dr. Jeffrey Rubin and Dr. Carol Rubin, *When Families Fight: How to Handle Conflict with Those You Love* (New York: William Morrow and Company, Inc., 1989), pp. 72, 64–67.

6. Cathi Hanauer, "Relating," *Seventeen*, July 1993, p. 76.

7. Rubin and Rubin, pp. 67–69.

8. Personal interview with Dr. Megan P. Goodwin, associate professor, Individual and Family Studies, Central Michigan University, Mt. Pleasant, Michigan, April 13, 1995.

9. Rubin and Rubin, p. 71.

10. Goodwin interview.

11. Platt interview.

Further Reading

*easier reading

Nonfiction
General

*Bode, Janet. *Truce: Ending the Sibling War*. New York: Dell Publishing Company, Inc., 1993.

Canter, Lee. *Surviving Sibling Rivalry*. Santa Monica, Calif.: Canter, Lee & Associates, 1994.

*Coleman, William L. *Getting Along With Brothers & Sisters*. Minneapolis: Augsburg Fortress Publishers, 1994.

Dunn, Judy. *From One Child to Two*. New York: Fawcett Book Group, 1995.

Dunn, Judy, and Robert Plomin. *Separate Lives: Why Siblings Are So Different*. New York: Basic Books, 1992.

Engelbreit, Mary. *There Is No Friend Like a Sister*. Lanham, Md.: Andrews & McMeel, 1993.

Faber, Adele, and Elaine Mazlish. *Siblings Without Rivalry: How to Help Your Children Live Together So You Can Live Too*. New York: Avon Books, 1988.

Fishel, Elizabeth. *Sisters: Shared Histories, Lifelong Ties*. Emeryville, Calif.: Conari Press, 1994.

Hapworth, William E., Mada Hapworth, and Joan R. Heilman. *Mom Loved You Best: Understanding Rivalry and Enriching Your Sibling Relationship*. New York: Viking Penguin, 1993.

*Landau, Elaine. *Sibling Rivalry: Brothers and Sisters at Odds*. Brookfield, Conn.: The Millbrook Press, Inc., 1994.

Mathias, Barbara. *Between Sisters: Secret Rivals, Intimate Friends*. New York: Delacorte Press, 1992.

McDermott, Patti. *Sisters and Brothers: Resolving Your Adult Sibling Relationships*. Los Angeles: Lowell House, 1993.

Reit, Seymour V. *Sibling Rivalry*. New York: Ballantine Books, Inc., 1988.

Saline, Carol. *Sisters*. Philadelphia: Running Press Book Publishers, 1994.

Samalin, Nancy, with Catherine Whitney. *Loving Each One Best: A Caring and Practical Approach to Raising Siblings*. New York: Bantam Books, 1996.

Sandmaier, Marian. *Original Kin: The Search for Connection among Adult Sisters and Brothers*. New York: Dutton, 1994.

★Senisi, Ellen B. *Brothers & Sisters*. New York: Scholastic, Inc., 1993.

Sunshine, Linda. *Mom Loves Me Best and Other Lies You Told Your Sister*. New York: Dutton, 1990.

Special Circumstances

Siblings with Special Needs:

★Brightman, A., and K. Storey. *Ginny*. New York: Scholastic's Feeling Free, 1978.

★McConnell, N. P., and N. Duell. *Different and Alike*. Colorado Springs: Current, Inc., 1982. (Overview of disabilities)

Rosenberg, Maxine B. *Finding A Way: Living with Exceptional Brothers and Sisters*. New York: Lothrop, Lee & Shepard, 1988.

Sibling or Parent Substance Abuse:

★*Alateen: Hope for Children of Alcoholics*. New York: Al-Anon Family Group Headquarters, Inc., 1992.

★McFarland, Rhoda. *Drugs and Your Brothers and Sisters*. Revised edition. New York: The Rosen Publishing Group, Inc., 1993.

Stepfamilies and Stepsiblings:

Bernstein, Anne C. *Yours, Mine and Ours: How Families Change When Remarried Parents Have a Child Together*. New York: W.W. Norton & Co. Inc., 1990.

★Getzoff, Ann, and Carolyn McClenahan. *Stepkids: A Survival Guide for Teenagers in Stepfamilies*. Lincoln, Neb.: Walker & Co., 1984.

Loss of a Sibling:

Croutharnel, Thomas G., Sr. *It's OK*. Second edition. Bradenton, Fla.: Keystone Press, 1990.

Rosen, Helen. *Unspoken Grief: Coping with Childhood Sibling Loss*. Lexington, Mass.: Lexington Books, 1986.

Fiction

*Adler, Carole S. *In Our House, Scott Is My Brother*. New York: Macmillan, 1980.

*Blume, Judy. *Here's To You, Rachel Robinson*. New York: Orchard Books, 1993.

*Blume, Judy. *Tales of a Fourth Grade Nothing*. New York: Dutton, 1972.

*Byars, Betsy. *The Night Swimmers*. New York: Delacorte Press, 1980.

*Cleaver, Vera and Bill. *The Kissimmee Kid*. (New York: Lothrop, Lee & Shepard Books, 1981.

*Colman, Hila. *The Family Trap*. New York: William Morrow, 1982.

*Fine, Anne. *The Book of the Banshee*. New York: Joy Street Books, 1992.

*Fox, Paula. *Western Wind*. New York: Orchard Books, 1993.

*Landis, James. *The Sisters Impossible*. New York: Knopf, distributed by Random House, 1979.

*Leigh, Frances. *The Lost Boy*. New York: Dutton, 1976.

*Lowry, Lois. *A Summer to Die*. Boston: Houghton Mifflin, 1977.

*McNair, Joseph. *Commander Coatrack Returns*. Boston: Houghton Mifflin, 1989.

*Matthews, Ellen. *Getting Rid of Roger*. Louisville: Westminster Press, 1978.

*Paterson, Katherine. *Jacob Have I Loved*. New York: Crowell, 1980.

*Pevsner, Stella. *And You Give Me a Pain, Elaine*. New York: Seabury Press, 1978.

*Pevsner, Stella. *Sister of the Quints*. New York: Clarion Books, 1987.

*Spinelli, Jerry. *Who Put That Hair in My Toothbrush?* New York: Little, Brown, 1984.

*Wright, Betty. *Ghosts Beneath Our Feet*. New York: Holiday House, 1984.

Answer Key

Test Your S.I.Q., *page 13*

Answers: All c's. If you answered all questions correctly, you have a healthy attitude toward your sibling. If you have mostly b's, you are too hard on yourself and others. If you missed more than three, then this book might help you take another look at your sibling relationship.

Friend or Foe?, *page 39*

Answers: 1-b; 2-c; 3-a; 4-c; 5-b; 6-c. If you got these right, you have good insight into the childhood foundation of sibling relationships.

What Would You Do?, *page 50*

If your answers were 1-c; 2-a; 3-b; 4-a; 5-a; 6-c, you've got a good handle on the teen years.

Friend or Fighter?, *page 75*

Answers: 1-c; 2-b; 3-a★; 4-b; 5-c; 6-c.
★Blame isn't constructive. If your feelings haven't changed after a few months, talk to your mother about getting help.

Index